HIDDEN HISTORY *of* ASHTABULA COUNTY

HIDDEN HISTORY *of* ASHTABULA COUNTY

Carl E. Feather

THE History PRESS

Published by The History Press
Charleston, SC 29403
www.historypress.net

First published 2015

Manufactured in the United States

ISBN 978.1.62619.953.8

Library of Congress Control Number: 2015938639

Notice: The information in this book is true and complete to the best of our knowledge. It is offered without guarantee on the part of the author or The History Press. The author and The History Press disclaim all liability in connection with the use of this book.

In honor of Dr. Richard and Norma Waters, Judy Pallutch and the late Walter Jack, my Ashtabula County history heroes, and my grandson, Mason L. Feather, on his ninth birthday: Learn well from the past, and the future will be your friend.

Contents

Acknowledgements

Writing a book is like coming down with the stomach flu. The demands that the task places on the infected author's time and energy eventually affect the entire household. At the very least, it is an inconvenience. At worst, it is an obsession that depletes the body, mind and soul. And so it is I start with an apology to my wife, Amanda, for the disruption to our lives that the time spent digging up *Hidden History of Ashtabula County* has caused. Thank you for bearing with me through what has been the longest winter of our lives and assisting in this project at every turn of its crooked course.

Much of this book was written with my black Labrador retriever at my feet, awaiting a walk but getting only prose and a pile of books and papers infringing on his space. Now that this manuscript is complete, it is my goal to make good on those promises of more walks.

Having acknowledged the household's contribution to this work, I will address the professionals'. I am indebted to the historians who came before me and had the wisdom to preserve the past while its details and words still hung from the branches of memory. Foremost is the late Walter Jack, whose prose is preserved in yellowed newspaper clippings from the *Jefferson Gazette*, *Erie Times* and *Ashtabula Star Beacon*. Many of these clips are on file in the library that bears his name at the Jennie Munger Gregory Memorial Museum at Geneva-on-the-Lake. Thank you Ashtabula County Historical Society members and volunteers for providing and maintaining this collection. And thank you, Norma Waters and other volunteers, for doing the same at the Jefferson Historical Society's research room.

Gratitude also goes to the Andover, Ashtabula County District and Kingsville Public Libraries and the Platt R. Spencer Archives & Special Collections Area.

Thank you to Neil Frieder, my former editor at the *Star Beacon*, who gave me the freedom to research and write about our local history during my decades of work under his direction.

Thank you, Krista Slavicek, acquisitions editor for The History Press, for all you did to bring this work to print.

And thank you to my parents, Carl J. and Cossette Feather, for their faith in me, their pride in what I do and the Appalachian heritage that is part of who I am. This book is as much theirs as it is mine. Thank you.

Introduction

I wrote this book while living in a small house on a quiet, dead-end street that starts in the city of Ashtabula, Ohio, and ends in Ashtabula Township. The street is one of several side lanes off Route 84, also known as the South Ridge.

I suspect that most of my neighbors are unaware of the human history hidden here and that few can explain the gaunt smokestacks that rise above the brown field just north of our ridge. No interpretive signage stands here, no stone monument honors the men who commissioned and paid for the cylindrical skyscrapers. The past owns them, and progress dictates that we pave over unprofitable history or take down that which was built to last forever.

The road in this section follows the path of the Old Girdled Road, which followed a trail that myriad Native Americans traveled through these parts of northeast Ohio. And before that? Some would suggest that a race of giants, possibly a lost tribe of Israel or a Scandinavian settlement, occupied this land by the thousands, based on the mysterious graves found on the township side of the Ashtabula River.

And what of those smokestacks? They mark the location of what was once a major industry, greenhouses, where everything from tomatoes to chrysanthemums grew under glass in a town known for its cold winters. That industry got its start here in 1880 when Frank Luce Sr. opened a greenhouse—or "hothouse," as they were called back then—for growing vegetables and flowers out of season. Other growers sprouted up in this same furrow: J.H. Rice, E.A. Dunbar, C.W. Hopkins, Lyle Blake, William Westcott, Yoder Brothers, the Mikkelsons and "Mushroom King" Roger

Griswold. His mushrooms embellished steaks served in the finest restaurants of East Coast cities while lettuce and tomatoes grown on the same flats provided salad for those establishments.

I like to poke around this abandoned property and look for clues to the past. I am not an archaeologist or a professional historian. But my aunt tells me that, when I was a kid, I drove the family bonkers with my constant "Why?" questions. I'm discontent with just the facts, which were what the eighth-grade history teacher was intent on teaching. That is not history. The facts must connect; I need to know why Roger Griswold was able to grow his mushrooms and others their lettuces and mums here and why the Girdled Road took the route it did. Most things don't just happen, especially when human effort and capital are being expended. Why did they do that? And why did it happen here? And why is the community the way it is?

And so I discover that this city could grow vegetables in the winter months because coal heated the greenhouses. The commodity was cheap and readily available from the Appalachian coal fields via rail. But competition from the trucking industry and increases in freight and energy costs stripped away this advantage, and the hothouses went cold, leaving a brownfield filled with artifacts and hidden history.

Yes, history is hidden, but what adventure there is in burrowing into its lair and fanning out into its musty labyrinth, flashlight and notepad in hand! So often the tunnels lead to nowhere but the beginning, and overturned stones hide nothing but common dirt. But the historian knows that history grows in both prosaic and extraordinary soil, and both require a modicum of patient attention to bring forth the story.

Lloyd R. Osborne, a historian who lived in the southern part of Ashtabula County, in 1932 boiled down more than 150 years of Pymatuning Valley history into a single map. "The historical details of significant importance in this particular section's life have had to be gleamed by laborious work, thru dusty books, thru millions of unimportant and insignificant words," wrote Osborne, who produced a very fine, concise map, indeed.

Hidden History of Ashtabula County comes after years of sifting through "millions of unimportant and insignificant words" and distilling therefrom articles for the Ashtabula *Star Beacon* newspaper. Most recently, I wrote the "Odd Tales of Ashtabula County" series to mark the 200th anniversary of the county's political organization (2011–12). What started as a weekly, one-year series became a two-year endeavor that could have gone on for as many more; one story led to another, and one intriguing sentence in a biography or newspaper clipping opened the door to another adventure.

The problem with anything of a serial nature, however, is that the reader seldom has the opportunity to hold the entire picture in his hands at once. Books like this, however, provide the venue for exploration and connection. Therefore, to those who faithfully followed the Odd Tales and other series in my journalism past, I apologize if this book does not meet their request for a collection of those articles in one place. Many of the stories will be found here, but they, like the history of which I write, will be "hidden" in the greater context.

I have purposely avoided writing about the Ashtabula County history that is familiar and spectacular. Specifically, the well-known Ashtabula Train Disaster will not be addressed. Likewise, I will leave discussion of the Civil War and Ashtabula County's Twenty-ninth Ohio Volunteer Infantry, the Giddings Regiment, to the recent, excellent works that give that important story the full breadth of which it is worthy.

Enough said. Let's go dig up some hidden history of Ashtabula County.

1
THE ROAD TO HISTORY

People prize old houses and public buildings for their "history"; we lament the fact that the walls can't talk and launch fundraising campaigns when progress threatens. Old roads, on the other hand, rarely rise to the same level of historical prominence. They are paved over, widened, intersected, overpassed, underpassed and abandoned as necessary to accommodate our appetite for speed, efficiency and convenience—a pity, for our old byways host history hidden in plain sight.

Properly interpreted, an old byway is a drive-it-yourself tour of local history. The astute traveler finds in its course and landmarks clues to historical events, eras, trends and migrations. He notices the architecture of the houses, especially those abandoned and decaying, and the design of the barns as keys to this timeline and the culture of its authors. He slows to read the sign posts and finds clues at every intersection and wide spot. The topography, and whether the road avoids or accommodates it, tells of the times and technology in which it was conceived. He pays attention to the denominations of the churches, the state of their structures and the size of their parking lots. He watches for repetition in the names on mailboxes. He looks for patterns and deviations. Even the road's moniker is a clue.

Stanhope-Kelloggsville Road is such a timeline. The byway originates in the northern section of the county at Kelloggsville in Monroe Township and heads south to the county line, where Trumbull County takes over and the byway becomes "State Road."

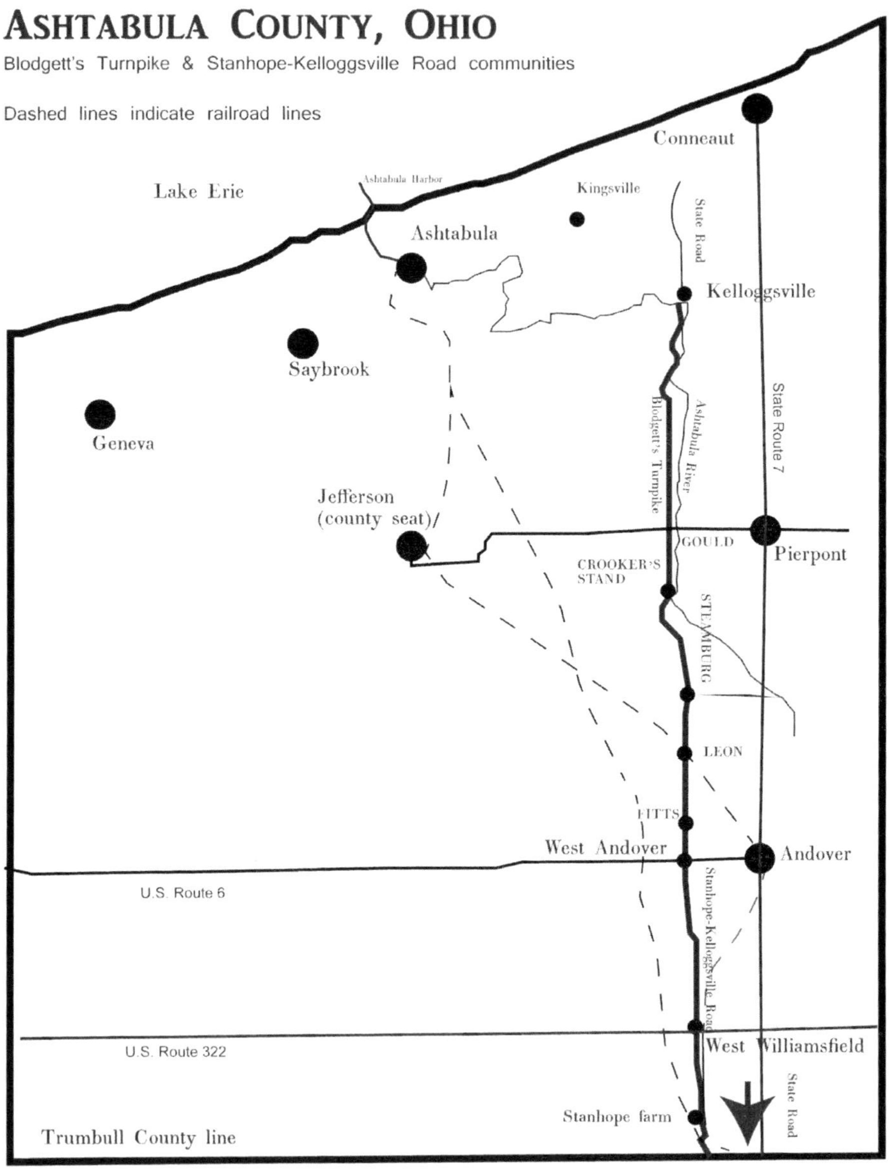

Blodgett's Turnpike was a section of the Stanhope-Kelloggsville (State) Road. Many small communities, most of them ghost towns today, sprang up along the route. *Author's collection.*

For part of its journey in Ashtabula County, the road straddles neighboring townships, doing double duty as a political boundary and two-lane transportation artery. It adopts the first part of its name from "Stanhope" in

Williamsfield Township, although, oddly enough, Stanhope was a station on the New York Central Railroad rather than a hamlet on the road. Its second part comes from an old town filled with hidden history.

OLD ROADS

Long before the first white man cut a road through what would become Kelloggsville, this area was a crossroads of trails worn into the landscape by the feet of Native Americans. The route these trails took was dictated by high ridges and the ease of crossing streams; it was at Kelloggsville that the west branch of the Ashtabula River was easily forded. Thus, when the Connecticut Land Company's Girdled Road was cut across Ashtabula County from the state line to Cleveland, the road passed through what was then known as Ferguson's Settlement but would soon become Kelloggsville.[1]

Although completed in late 1797, the Girdled Road did not bring an immediate influx of settlers. Hardship and natural enemies awaited any person with the goal of settling this land. William Hardy arrived here in 1803 from Mifflin County, Pennsylvania, with ten sheep and as many hogs. The bears ate the hogs, and the wolves killed his sheep. Bears and coons destroyed his four acres of corn. The land, poorly drained and dense with forest, was equally challenging.

This landscape awaited the right man for the job, and that man was Caleb Blodgett (1786–1840).[2] A Vermont native, Blodgett arrived in the county circa 1810. He purchased fifty acres in the northwest area of what would become Kelloggsville and settled there. A young man of great ambition with the energy to match, Blodgett sought complementary investments and ventures. Soon after arriving in Kelloggsville, he purchased the distillery built by Jacob Paden and William Frazier. Blodgett would build five more distilleries, plus a brewery, in the community.

As in other parts of the frontier, it was much more efficient to transport a finished product, whiskey, than the raw corn. Whiskey also served as a form of currency; even pastors of the frontier churches were partially compensated in alcohol in an economy where cash was scarce.

Blodgett recognized that Kelloggsville was well suited for hospitality businesses, such as distilleries and taverns. In 1811, he built the community's first frame house for the Benson family, but its raison d'être was to be a tavern that catered to stagecoach passengers. One such line connected Erie,

Pennsylvania, to Pittsburgh and passed through the hamlet. Blodgett was an investor in that line, as well as one between Buffalo and Cleveland. Seeing the potential that these lines held for the growth of the community and his business interests, Blodgett promoted construction of a turnpike between Kelloggsville and the southern section of Richmond Township, a distance of fifteen miles.

Blodgett's Turnpike,[3] as it became known, was a "corduroy road"; it was built from logs laid side by side with the gaps filled with dirt. Rain and snow washed out or turned the dirt to mud, and any wheeled conveyance went "bump-bump" as it traveled the toll road. In addition to the toll of misery this turnpike took on travelers and teams, there was a monetary toll to pay. At Kelloggsville, the tollgate was erected between two poplar trees.

Blodgett melded his distillery, stagecoach and turnpike interests in his tavern. The frame structure was replaced by a brick one in 1824 to accommodate the ever-increasing influx of travelers and commerce. The second floor of this tavern was a dance hall, and the first floor provided sustenance and refreshment. Stables were out back.

Blodgett's business prospered. It is said that lodging was so scarce in Kelloggsville, travelers and teamsters alike slept on bedrolls spread out on

Caleb Blodgett built his tavern in Kelloggsville in 1824. The stately structure is now a private residence on the Stanhope-Kelloggsville Road. *Author photograph.*

the barroom floor, although one must wonder if this was the result of a dearth of lodging or the strength and abundance of Blodgett's distilled spirits. Eventually, fourteen hotels and taverns were built in the vicinity of the turnpike's northern terminus. Blodgett, ever the opportunist, even built one for a competitor, directly across the turnpike from his.[4]

These were heady days for Kelloggsville, which, for a short while, had a population larger than the Girdled Road's western terminus, Cleveland. During the decade of 1820–30, Ashtabula County's population doubled to more than fourteen thousand.[5] At virtually every meeting of the county's board of commissioners, petitions for new roads and bridges, as well as reports of surveyors, were heard. Many of these early roads were created to link a mill or tannery to a population center or port. The first road from Kelloggsville, for example, went north from the settlement to Paden's Mills at the waterfall. It went on to ford the creek and eventually reached the south and north ridge roads. Essentially an extension of Blodgett's Turnpike, the road remains as State Road.

Blodgett believed in diversification of his business interests. He built the first tannery in Kelloggsville and, for five years, had the contract to supply meat to the garrison at Green Bay. He still found time to be a father and husband. At least one child, Sarepta Marie,[6] was born to Chloe (Kidder) and Caleb Blodgett while they lived in Monroe Township.

Blodgett was "a man who assumed great risks, and many times would be unable to meet his obligations," according to the Williams brothers' *History of Ashtabula County*. In order to evade his creditors at stage stations, Blodgett hid in a boiler being transported from Pittsburgh to Kelloggsville. And he was nearly kidnapped by a party determined to return him to Batavia, New York, where a bail bond awaited.

It is unfortunate that Blodgett, who did much to build Kelloggsville, was not honored when it came time to change the hamlet's name from its original "Ferguson's Settlement." That name was a nod to the three Ferguson brothers who purchased 200 acres at the site of the present-day village. New Englander Martin Kellogg came to the hamlet by way of Virginia in 1813 and his brother, Amos, the following year. The Kellogg brothers purchased the Ferguson brothers' land and another 640 acres north of town. The name was soon changed to Kelloggsville.

Blodgett would have to be satisfied with having a turnpike named after him, although that name, too, gave way to a different moniker after the road was extended. He could, however, take pride in the fact that his road was mother to a number of other communities south of Kelloggsville.[7]

FROM GOULD TO STANHOPE

Walter Jack grew up in Pierpont Township and, as a young man, listened to the stories passed down from the old pioneer settlers. As an adult, Jack wrote extensively about the history of Ashtabula County and Northwest Pennsylvania. His recollections include those of Gould and Drs. Brayman and Anderson. *Ashtabula County Historical Society collection.*

The old turnpike's course was dictated by the west branch of the Ashtabula River, and if the river deviated from its generally north–south course, as it does in the northwest corner of Richmond Township, so did the road. It was less costly to stay on the high ridge and build the road around the loop than to take the shorter route of building and maintaining two bridges.

Economic opportunity, and thus hamlets, was born wherever an east–west road encountered the turnpike. A road that connected the state line to the county seat of Jefferson fostered the growth of Gould, about three miles west of Pierpont Center. Gould's namesake was Archibald Gould, but the post office was named Phoenix. It first appears on a county map in 1873.

Old-timers who recalled this area before all the timber was cleared said that the hemlock/pine forest was so thick "one could not see his hand before him on a bright summer day." The forest also was a refuge for horse thieves, who made use of the community's proximity to the state line, as well.

Out of the need to thwart this activity came the Order of State Police, aka Anti-Horse Thief Society or Horse Police, which organized into lodges or camps of the Grand Encampment. Working with a similar organization in Pennsylvania, camps in Monroe, Pierpont, Penn Line and several other Ashtabula County communities confronted horse-theft rings in the region. Due to the large, thick forests on both sides of the state line, the membership of the group was quite inclusive, at least as far as the "respectable" citizenry goes. The Monroe Township group disbanded in the early 1920s. By then, much of the forest had been cleared, and folks just weren't using horses like they once did.

During the years that the forests were being cut, hamlets like Gould flourished. Timber was their lifeblood. At its zenith, Gould had sawmills, two

This old house at Gould, shown in a mid-twentieth-century photograph by Walter Jack, was once a hotel. *Ashtabula County Historical Society collection.*

stores, two churches, a hotel, a covered bridge and a water system—a town pump. It also had a horse racetrack, owned by Dr. L.E. Brayman, a Pierpont Township physician who owned a large farm and specialized in racehorses.

Gould even had a dentist, "Doc Everets," who practiced in a corner room of an old house. In those days, one did not need a medical degree to practice dentistry. Everets had been a teacher and preacher before taking up dentistry as a way to ease the suffering of mankind. He used oil of cloves to numb the pain and was known for his skill in handling both his instruments and patients' anxieties. A filling cost a quarter and an extraction fifty cents.

In the mid-1920s, the road between Jefferson and Pierpont was rerouted, and Gould was bypassed. The town began to fade away: the covered bridge, store, hotel, dentist—all gone. Nevertheless, there is a cemetery that is reached by Gould Road, which is grassed over and appropriately dead-ends at the burial grounds.

Next on this line was "Crooker's Stand," a pioneer-days hotel for turnpike travelers. The hostelry's fame was said to be known from "Kentucky to Canada" during the Mexican War (1846–48) era. The community stood where South Denmark Road connects to Stanhope-Kelloggsville Road.

The cemetery at Gould is all that remains of the little hamlet that was well known and visited for its dentist, "Doc Everets." *Walter Jack/Ashtabula County Historical Society collection.*

Laurys Fee, in an article that appeared in *Regional Press*, the magazine of the *Star-Beacon*, said Crooker's Stand got its name from the "crooks" who frequented the place. The few accounts and recollections of Crooker's Stand suggest that it was a rowdy spot where cheap whiskey and perhaps a few other vices abounded.

Walter Jack preserved this anecdote from Crooker's Stand:

> *Merald Haines of Denmark, who had the story handed down to him from his father Jim Haines told the writer that the Crooker Stand was a going concern years before the Civil War and was quite a meeting place for men round about where whiskey was twenty-five or thirty cents per gallon and keg and contents may have been bought from the distillery at Kelloggsville. Merald told of one night when the boys took over the bar room bringing in a cross-legged saw horse, another bored a hole in the bottom of the keg, driving in a spigot and it was swung on the horse. One of the crowd mounted astride the keg waving his hands, "Come on boys, whiskey from*

this end of the barrel ten cents a tin cup full and from the other end five cents." They seemed to relish the psychology of the situation, trying first one end and then the other and would agree that it was really better from the ten cent end and worth the difference.

STEAMBURG

The next mile and half of this road was known, collectively, as Steamburg. The town officially terminated just south of where the Jefferson-Meadville (Pennsylvania) highway connected with the turnpike. Steamburg is still noted on the county map, although no sign or building marks its spot.

Steamburg also marked the end of Blodgett's Turnpike. From this point south, it became known as "State Road" or the "Old Salt Road," but for clarity and continuity, we'll continue to refer to it by its present-day name, "Stanhope-Kelloggsville."

As for Steamburg's moniker, the late Walter Jack's account of the "Romantic Old Turnpike" attributes it to a steam-powered sawmill built at this location. The name of "Old Corey" Sheldon is connected with the mill and Steamburg's first recorded tragedy: around 1853, the boiler exploded, and Sheldon was killed.

"Neighbors hurried to the scene and among those were the grandparents [of Walter Jack], who were close friends of the Sheldons even though both had been in the neighborhood but a short time," Walter Jack wrote. "The tragedy of the boiler explosion was long remembered in the community and frequently spoken of for half a century."

There were "row on row of wooden buildings" at Steamburg, as well as a church, school and post office. The timber industry flourished here from 1840 to 1890. During the winter months, when the stream froze over, the logs were hauled into the valley and piled onto the ice. When the ice finally thawed and the stream ran high, the logs would float into the millpond.

"The old up-and-down…saw was used," Walter Jack wrote. "The saw was suspended in a frame the size of a barn door. The log progressed through the frame. Saw and frame arose with the upstroke of the pitman (connecting rod) from the water wheel. The down stroke of this saw, which looked much like an over-thick crosscut, did the cutting." Just two or three men could saw three to four thousand board feet of lumber with one of these mills in just one day. Part of this efficiency was due to the abundance of "white wood," or yellow poplar, which was relatively easy to cut.

Further, an efficient waterwheel design that eliminated the need for a high dam and long millrace was developed along the millstreams of Ashtabula County. V.N. Orsmsby of Pierpont spent most of his life working around the sawmills of the county, and he told Walter Jack that the wheel was "on the order of a four blade propeller. This was enclosed, and the force of the water going through provided power through shaft and pitman to the saw… The water wheel was cut out with an adz and the curvature of the blades was important."

Standing beside this lazy stream on a summer day, it is hard to imagine that it once had adequate flow to support so many mills. Indeed, even back then, the locals referred to this branch of the Ashtabula River as a "creek" rather than a river. The reason the stream could maintain a steady flow throughout the year was because the forest slowly released water to the creek; as the land was cleared, the water levels fluctuated wildly.

Nevertheless, in those pioneer days, some dreamers envisioned vessels from Lake Erie making their way up the Ashtabula River and west branch to Steamburg.

Abel Mead banked on this concept when he attempted to sell prime "riverfront" real estate in northwest Richmond Township to outsiders.[8] Mead was postmaster of "Steamburg," and Walter Jack's story of the scam has him married to a Georgia woman much younger than Mead and desiring to reclaim some of the wealth that her family lost in the Civil War. Alas, the poor lady was ill prepared for the culture, or lack thereof, in rural Ashtabula County, as well as her husband's chicanery.

Mead's plan was to convince investors that the west branch of the Ashtabula was navigable all the way to Lake Erie and would provide a boom to Richmond Township, certain to become a major port on the river. His chief sales tool was a map as large as his dining table.

Ashtabula County recorder and historian Paul Hakala interviewed a Wesley Kyle for his 1968 story on Steamburg. Kyle claimed to have seen one of the maps. "There was a real town plotted, and on the west branch of the Ashtabula Creek were to be seen in dock three large-masted schooners awaiting their cargoes. There was to be seen the hotel, the church, the post office…The West Branch of the Ashtabula was shown in a stream capable of accommodating the largest of the lake vessels," Hakala wrote.

Mead struck purchase deals with Steamburg property owners just in case he successfully convinced the unwary of the west branch's maritime potential. That led to litigation when Mead could not live up to his side of the bargain. And Hakala wrote that a family in Buffalo bought Mead's story and traded some valuable real estate for Steamburg lots.

After being run out of Ashtabula County, Mead moved to Michigan, where once again dabbled in real estate schemes. His southern wife grew tired of these broken promises, and she returned to Georgia, penniless.[9]

Leon United Methodist Church and a few houses are all that remain of a community that, prior to World War I, had one of the largest milk shipping plants in the county. A store, sawmill, tavern and depot once stood here. *Author's collection.*

Steamburg also was the home of John Harvey, whose pre-Steamburg exploits included being captain on a canalboat and stock farming. By the time he reached Steamburg, where he lived in a former schoolhouse, Harvey was a broken man—literally. He had been tossed from a buggy and remained handicapped for the rest of his life. Nevertheless, Harvey grafted apple trees, doctored sick animals, concocted "Green Mountain Salve" and invented an extension ladder. Separated from his wife and destitute, Harvey nevertheless made quite an impression on his neighbors as a natural healer with an unnaturally powerful odor.

Harvey developed a large, malignant tumor, which he treated with one of his home remedies. To the surprise of his neighbors, and physician Dr. Brayman, the tumor shriveled up. Brayman offered Harvey "three figures" for the cure, but Harvey refused to sell it. He did offer it to others afflicted with the disease, but it's said that his "unkept, smelly appearance…broke down their confidence."

LEON

Amid these stories of hamlets built of timber and turnpike is an anomaly, Leon, which owed its glory days to the milk and railroads rather than a corduroy road.

While Abel Mead used the Lake Erie–Ohio River transportation link as a scam, men of greater industry and scruples sought to link the waterways with rails.

"The minds of leading men of the county were at an early day awakened to the importance of connecting the Ohio river and the lake by a railroad," states the Williams brothers' *History of Ashtabula County.* Routes were studied, corporations formed and shares issued, but for one reason or another, construction did not get underway until the early 1870s.

When the logjam finally broke, two competing north–south railroads were built in as many years. The first railroad to reach Ashtabula Harbor on Lake Erie was the Pittsburgh, Youngstown and Ashtabula (PY&A), which opened to traffic on May 1, 1873. This rail line terminated on the west side of the Ashtabula River and passed through Austinburg and Rock Creek on its way south to Trumbull County. The line became part of the Penn Central system and eventually was abandoned. Its bed was repurposed as the Western Reserve Greenway Trail, a multi-use recreation trail.

The Lake Shore & Michigan Southern (LS&MS) already had a strong presence in Ashtabula County when the PY&A arrived at Ashtabula Harbor. The Cleveland, Painesville and Ashtabula, a forerunner to the LS&MS, was completed in 1852 and linked Ashtabula to Cleveland. The eastern portion of the railroad was completed in 1853. Thus, the northern villages were linked by railroad to cities to the east and west; the stagecoach business plummeted, as did shipping from Ashtabula Harbor. No longer did merchants and passengers have to depend on the schooners and Lake Erie's temperament for their goods and travel. The impact on shipping was immediate and devastating. Prior to the railroads, more than 500 vessels entered and departed from this port annually. By 1870, the number had fallen to 114.

The two north–south railroads, which competed for business, would awaken the harbor from its doldrums. Driving this revival and the rush to build these railroads were the steel manufacturing industries of the Ohio and Mahoning Valleys and the discovery of iron ore in the Mesabi Range of the Upper Great Lakes region. During the 1850s, mining and shipping infrastructure was built to provide a cost-effective way of getting the ore onto vessels headed for lower-lake ports. Ashtabula Harbor was a prime receiving port for this ore, offering the shortest distance between Lake Erie and the steel mills of the aforementioned regions. By the early 1870s, the stage was

The coming of the railroads to Ashtabula Harbor provided a conduit for iron ore to reach the steel mills of the Ohio River Valley. This development spurred the immigration of Finnish, Italian, Swedish and other foreign workers to Ashtabula. *Ashtabula County Historical Society collection.*

set for Lake Erie ports and river-town steel mills, along with any town that would end up along these north–south rail lines, to prosper.

Competition was very keen among the county's villages and hamlets to attract a rail route through the community. The LS&MS chose for its "Franklin Route" a path that went from the lake port to Jefferson and then in a southeasterly direction to Andover. Just south of the village, the railroad split into two divisions: the Mahoning Coal & Coke Railroad, which finally achieved that connection between Lake Erie and the Mahoning Valley, and the Ashtabula & Franklin Branch, which veered to the east and the coal fields of Pennsylvania.

Kelloggsville, once the busiest little hamlet in Ashtabula County, was bypassed by the railroad. However, the Mahoning Coal & Coke Railroad and Ashtabula & Jamestown Branch paid homage to Stanhope-Kelloggsville Road farther south at Leon Station, in the far southwest corner of Richmond Township.

Before the railroad, this hamlet was known as Barber's Stand, a reference to P. Merriman Barber, who owned hundreds of acres of land in Richmond and Dorset Townships. Barber's Stand had a general store, a trading station and several taverns. In 1836, Barber became postmaster of the first post office in Richmond Township, Barber's Stand. The post office was located in his house.

Barber believed in the orderly development of a hamlet, and he subdivided an area known as "Leon Square" into half-acre building lots. When the railroad arrived, Leon already had a hotel and store on the tidy square. The community earned the investment of a depot, thanks to another Barber innovation—a cheese factory that employed twelve persons and turned out three tons of curd daily. It also helped that Barber felt it his civic duty to donate the land for the depot. A dance hall was built on the depot's second floor by Barber's son-in-law, Albert N. Slater. A stockyard, a creamery, a butter factory and more taverns followed.

Perhaps the most impressive feature of Leon was the sidewalk. It was two thousand feet long and stretched from the hotel to the church. James Weston Peebles operated a sawmill near the railroad tracks and donated the planks for the walkway. Peebles, in addition to being a generous Christian, was quite the family man. He had fourteen children and a penchant for naming them after prominent Democrats.

He thus had a son named Grover and promised that if Grover Cleveland won the election, he would let the sawmill whistle blow continually for a month. After the results reached Leon, Peebles made good on his promise.

Alas, the sparks from a passing train, perhaps with a Republican crew, fell onto the mill and caused a fire that mercifully cut short Peebles's promise.

Between the cheese, butter, lumber and livestock, Leon had grown to become the largest shipping center in Ashtabula County by 1899. The decline thereafter was rapid. The cheese factory was torn down, and over the decades, fire destroyed the tavern, several barns and a hotel-turned-house. Eventually, the train no longer stopped at Leon, and the tracks were gone by 1960.

FITTS

About one mile north of West Andover where a little spring-fed stream wanders from Stanhope-Kelloggsville to Creek Road was an industrial area where two gristmills, a distillery and a woolen mill took their power from an overshot wheel driven by the impounded water of the brook.

An ashery also was built here. Ashes collected from the piles of timber burned as a result of clearing the land were collected in barrels. Water from the stream was passed through these to extract the potassium hydroxide and potassium carbonate in the ashes. The lye solution thus obtained was used for making soap from fats. The water also could be evaporated to produce potash.

The woolen mill was built in 1824 by Case and Slater. In 1848, it was sold to A.D. Clifford, whose employees finished the yarn that women, working in their homes, spun from the wool fibers. The mill produced "fulled cloth," wool beaten and shrunk to a width of twenty-seven inches. The cloth was then spread over a table, and workers sprayed skim milk, without a single particle of cream or fat, onto the material. The means of spraying were simple and crude: the workers filled their mouths with milk and blew it onto the fabric. The moistened fabric then went into a press utilizing hot iron plates.

Clifford's factory burned in 1862, but he rebuilt. In 1866, the factory was sold to C.H. Fitts of Kinsman. Fitts was an experienced wool manufacturer, and he gradually updated the factory with power looms and other new machinery. The little mill employed young women at the pay rate of twenty-four dollars per month to operate the power looms. Farmers from the region who raised sheep brought their wool to the mill to sell or have it carded for the lady of the home to spin and knit.

Fitts Mill is long gone, but the impounded stream that powered the woolen mill and other industries in this area along Stanhope-Kelloggsville Road is still visible. *Author's collection.*

The Fitts woolen mill on Stanhope-Kelloggsville Road was one of several factories in an area where a stream was impounded to provide water power. *Williams Brothers History of Ashtabula County.*

Fitts Mill gained a reputation for producing fine woolen goods dyed with both natural dyes, such as cochineal bugs for red and blue from logwood, and the dyes derived from coal tar. Thousands of yards of checked and plaid goods were produced by the mill. Everything from shirts and dresses to underwear were made from this fine fabric. Toward the end of the mill's history, blankets became its specialty, and in one year, more than 1,500 pairs of them were produced for retailers of quality goods. (Blankets were sold as "pairs" at the time because the weaving process resulted in one common side; if the buyer's needs dictated, he could cut the "pair" in half and have two blankets.)

The sound of the shuttle and whirl of the spinning wheel loom were silenced in 1903. The industries that once flourished along this little brook fell into disrepair, or their buildings were repurposed. Water coming forth from the spring and feeding the little brook is the only constant at what was once known as "Fitts' Corners."

The eastern edge of Andover Township was swampy and difficult to settle, but the western side, especially along the turnpike, was blessed with higher ground, timber and fresh water. Thus, West Andover, which stands at the intersection of present-day Route 6 and Stanhope-Kelloggsville Road, became the early epicenter of the township.

By 1814, the hamlet had its first school, post office and wedding ceremony. The center shifted to the east when the Franklin Division of the LS&MS Railroad snubbed West Andover for Sharon, or Andover Village, as it would become known. Businesses followed the railroad and never came back; a solitary tavern marks the crossroads today.

Fort Ann, a place long gone from the map and highway, was south of West Andover on Stanhope-Kelloggsville Road. The "fort" reportedly was named after Fort Ann, New York, from which its first settlers hailed. The crossroads once had two churches, a store, a school and a tobacco factory. Joe Baker,[10] a pioneer businessman in Andover, owned the factory, as well as a store in Andover where he sold his tobacco. Baker also served as Andover Township clerk for more than fifty years.

Just as Blodgett's Tavern offered repose in Kellogsville, at the intersection of Stanhope-Kelloggsville and present-day Route 322 (West Williamsfield), there once stood a cupola-topped hotel known as the "Eagle." The owners, the Ford family, were Democrats—very strong Democrats—in a Republican stronghold.

Debating politics was a popular pastime at the hotel, and the debates got very stormy. On one occasion, an impassioned speaker picked up the

A postcard of the C.B. Stanhope store in West Williamsfield. The Stanhope family was entrusted with a quantity of coffee that Captain Charles R. Stanhope brought back from Cuba during his seafaring days. The coffee was kept in the family for more than eight decades. *Ashtabula County Historical Society collection.*

heating stove and tossed it through a window to make a point. There was contention over the flagpole in the front of the hotel, as well; the owners' enemies kept drilling holes in it until it was so weak it could not support the colors. And whoever built the hotel misjudged the distance from the road. The front porch extended into the road right-of-way, and travelers would ride their horses through the porch, perhaps to make a point.

The hotel and its highway obstruction went up in flames in 1916.

STANHOPE

Stanhope marks the end of this old road in Ashtabula County, although the byway continues to Kinsman in Trumbull County as "State Road." Captain John Rider Stanhope (1791–1873), a seaman, ship owner and builder of considerable note, owned the land north of the county line and imparted his surname to this land.

Stanhope launched his sailing career out of Newport, Rhode Island, in the early 1800s. The captain eventually tired of the seafaring life and,

Philip John Stanhope still farms a portion of the Captain John Stanhope farm in Williamsfield Township. This house was built in 1896 by William H. Stanhope using proceeds from selling a racehorse. *Author's collection.*

at the age of sixty, moved to his property at Williamsfield with his wife, Harriet Cornell, whom he married in 1816. Harriet's family started Cornell University; Captain Stanhope's lineage was the historic English house of Stanhope. His ancestor was Philip Dormer Stanhope, Earl of Chesterfield.

Captain Stanhope built a large house for his family and all the treasures he'd acquired during his years of sailing the world. The gently rolling acreage became known as Burnside, a dairy farm and preserve for livestock from around the world: Cuban cattle, hairless sheep, Hamburg geese. An accidental fire destroyed the captain's first house and all his treasures. He rebuilt and, on each corner of the front terrace, placed a stone swan fountain. That house has since passed from the scene, as well.

One must veer off to the west and onto Stanhope Lane to reach what remains of the family farm,[11] which is owned by Philip John Stanhope, whose great-great-great-grandfather was Captain Stanhope. Just below this estate are a gulley and a fine stone culvert that appears to be under Stanhope-Kelloggsville Road. That is an illusion; the culvert is actually under the former Mahoning Coal & Coke Road rail bed.

A handsome culvert on the Stanhope farm marks the spot where the railroad crossed the farm and the site of the cheese factory. The rails and factory are long gone. *Author's collection.*

The home in which Philip John lives was built in 1896 by his great-grandfather William Henry Stanhope. To fund the construction, his great-grandfather sold some racehorses from the farm.

A neighbor tells me that if you know where to look, you can make out the foundation of the Burnside Cheese Factory, which was serviced by this extinct railroad and stood across the road from Philip's farm.

The Burnside factory was purchased by the Reich Company and expanded in the early 1900s. It was one of numerous cheese factories built along Stanhope-Kelloggsville Road. Dairy was a prominent industry in nineteenth-century Ashtabula County, and the highest-volume cheese factory in the world, at least in 1880, stood to the west of Stanhope-Kelloggsville Road, south of West Andover.

The county's fame as a cheese-producing area was sealed in 1876 when several factories joined forces with the railroad in a "publicity stunt." The occasion was the Philadelphia Centennial, which celebrated the 100th anniversary of the nation's founding. On exhibit, there was the "Big Cheese from Ashtabula County." The weight of this hunk was 2,300 pounds. It was so large it could not fit through the door of a boxcar (so much for planning) and had to be transported on a railroad flat car. To protect it from the

The cheese factory at West Andover was one of the largest in the county. *Andover Public Library collection.*

weather, a tent was erected over the cheese. Several men accompanied the cargo to Philadelphia and camped under the tent en route.

This mega curd required the entire day's output of "firm-cheese" curd from five factories: West Andover, Cherry Valley, Wayne, Pierpont and Mineral Springs (Trumbull County). Pressed into a custom-built mold, the cheese was used as an advertisement for Ashtabula County's dairy industry. The stunt paid for itself, too. Toward the end of the exposition, chunks were cut off and sold. "In a very short time it was all disposed of and the men returned home with the cash," wrote Charles S. Denslow of Saybrook Township, who worked for the New York Central Railroad and had a hand in the project.

The big cheese had a predecessor from Ashtabula County. In 1840, on the farm of James Stone in Morgan County, a large cheese made from curd contributed by area farmers was crafted, tended and prepared for shipment. The recipient was Queen Victoria. Stone, who was a publicity hound, also made a 1,900-pound cheese that was awarded the silver cup by the American Institute in New York in 1848.

The production of cheese produced several byproducts, which were processed in other buildings or fed to livestock. This image is of the milk sugar factory at West Andover. *Andover Public Library collection.*

Cheese factories often produced their own containers at the factory. Basswood, harvested from the forests of Ashtabula County, was preferred for the thin sheets of wood that were fashioned into containers by the factories.

The cheese factories also spun off other industries that used the byproducts. One of these was milk sugar, which could be crystalized and ground into a powder. Casein, another byproduct, was a good hog feed. Most of the cheese factories had a hog pen where they fattened the hogs on the byproducts. A typical cheese factory could send fifty hogs to market annually.

The county produced 5.49 million tons of cheese in 1849, about 25 percent of all cheese produced in Ohio. While the gross numbers fell in ensuing decades, Ashtabula County's cheese industry was among the first county industries to produce a product for export in any significant quality.

"This is the banner county of the State in the production of butter and cheese, while it ranks low in the amount it yields of wheat, corn and oats," observed the Williams brothers' *History of Ashtabula County.*

In 1875, the county also led the region in production of butter with just over one million pounds.[12]

Ashtabula County's cheese economy operated as part of the greater Western Reserve dairy industry. Beginning in 1815, the Western Reserve began a steady rise to prominence in the cheese market. As early as 1816, the dairy farmers of the Reserve had a near monopoly on the cheese market at Pittsburgh. The market expanded to the Ohio Valley and, from there, to California, New York City and even China, according to *History of Agriculture in Ohio* by Robert Leslie Jones.

It must be remembered that this quantity of production was performed not by a few "factory farms" but by hundreds of small farms, each with an average of forty to sixty cows. A single factory at Eagleville consumed the milk of one thousand cows. The output was so great that the wastewater from the plant polluted the nearby Mill Creek. The railroad drew its water for the locomotives from this creek, and when the stream's natural flow was insufficient to dilute the cheese factory's contribution, the water foamed in the boilers and the locomotives stalled at a nearby grade.

In what was perhaps an extreme case of poetic justice, the railroads contributed to the demise of the county's cheese industry in the early twentieth century. Demand and prices for the fluid milk rose in the large cities. And because railroads offered rapid transport of this milk from producers to consumer, it was no longer necessary to convert the excess to

The Amish have made good use of the old barns and farmhouses along the southern end of Stanhope-Kelloggsville Road in Williamsfield Township. *Author's collection.*

Stanhope-Kelloggsville Road has a number of Amish farms along its northern section. They represent the next step in the evolution of this old byway, which was cut through wilderness from Lake Erie to Kinsman more than two hundred years ago. *Author's collection.*

cheese. Tanker cars replaced the boxcars that hauled the cheese, and the old factories went out of business.

Today, there is but one cheese "factory" in Ashtabula County. A boutique cheese operation on the east side of Orwell, Mayfield Road Creamery has kept producing cheese long after most of the county's other dairy farms have been converted to grain operations.

There remain along Stanhope-Kelloggsville Road iconic silos of these former dairy concerns, but the farming here is mostly grain, beef cattle and perch. Even Philip Stanhope, whose ancestors supplied milk to the cheese factories of Stanhope-Kelloggsville Road, sold off his dairy herd in September 2014. While he plans to raise some beef cattle on the 260 acres that remain of the original 640, Philip, in his early sixties, recognizes that his body simply is not up to the physical demands of dairy farming.

For the Amish of western New York and northwestern Pennsylvania, however, the lightly used farmland and tired farmhouses of Stanhope-Kelloggsville Road offer a relatively inexpensive entry into a life lived close to the land. Beginning in the early 1990s, families arrived by the dozens from settlements in New York and Geauga County, built their schoolhouses, repaired the farmhouses, erected barns with red metal siding and practiced their agrarian traditions and faith.

With the Amish influx, Blodgett's Turnpike came full circle. Today, as was the case two hundred years ago, horse-drawn conveyances travel the byway. Those who pay the gasoline tax ante up for the "toll."

The horse-drawn buggies that ply the old turnpike are outward signs of a value system and a narrow interpretation of the Christian scriptures. As these buggies carry their adherents to worship in the homes around the settlement, they pass "Yankee" versions of this same faith. Regardless of the version, this much remains constant: faith transforms people, builds communities and drives events, including the settlement of a new world and civil wars. And like roads, faith has a way of hiding history in plain sight.

2
FAITH

Ashtabula County was as strongly influenced by its New England origin in religion as in anything else. The churches of the county were either Congregational or Presbyterian until the nineteenth century had reached its first quarter.
—*John Struthers Stewart,* History of Northeastern Ohio

Settled primarily by New Englanders, the Western Reserve was as fertile ground for souls as it was for crops and new beginnings. Two-thirds of the original settlers in Ashtabula County were from Connecticut, although elsewhere in the Reserve the mix was less than 50 percent. Just as there were no stores, barns, bridges or homes awaiting the settlers, there were no houses of worship except as God provided in nature. But for Puritanism's faithful remnant in New England, New Connecticut brought a fresh opportunity to redeem the vision of a New Zion that had failed to play out in the colonies.

Settlement of the Western Reserve also coincided with the era of the Second Great Awakening, a virtually nationwide revival that took the original Great Awakening of the 1730s and early 1740s beyond the New England colonies and into the backcountry. The awakening stirred the spirit of evangelism wherever the circuit riders of Methodism and lay pastors of the Baptist tradition found a stump on which to deliver their warnings of hell and hope of salvation

Ashtabula County would experience this "moving of the Spirit," much to the chagrin of missionaries from those denominations that emphasized an intellectual, rather than emotional, response to the gospel.

First Congregational Church in Ashtabula came out of First Presbyterian in 1860 due to a disagreement over the slavery issue. The pastor and part of the congregation held a proslavery view, resulting in the withdrawal of sixty people who organized the new congregation. The building was dedicated in 1862; this photograph shows it prior to a lightning strike that destroyed the tall steeple. *Ashtabula County Historical Society collection.*

Of the former camp was Reverend Joseph Badger, one of four missionaries dispatched by the Connecticut Missionary Society to the Western Reserve. This society officially formed on June 21, 1798, although it had existed for decades as the General Association of Connecticut, whose purpose was to "extend Congregational piety and order in the wilderness," writes Amy DeRogartis in *Moral Geography: Maps, Missionaries and the American Frontier*.

The challenge facing this group was finding men of God with the physical stamina, spiritual dedication and willingness to live in poverty and wilderness to the glory of God. Badger agreed to become such a martyr and was one to remind his commissioning society of this sacrifice. Alas, he fell short of the example set by the faith's humble servant David Brainerd, who used his physical and spiritual trials on the frontier to sharpen his holiness. He became the poster child for the suffering missionary to the Native Americans and other lost souls, a spiritual "case study" in "disinterested benevolence," whose pursuit of holiness was honored in his biography, *Life of Brainerd*.

Badger also left behind a tome, a memoir in which he shared the many hardships that he and his family suffered, in part, due to the stinginess and unrealistic expectations of his bosses back in Old Connecticut.

A Yale-educated Congregationalist, Revolutionary War veteran and Federalist, Badger was mature and with a family when he accepted the

Reverend Joseph Badger faced great hardships while doing God's work in the Western Reserve. His work led to the establishment of several Congregational and Presbyterian churches in Ashtabula County. *Author's collection.*

call. His first tour of the Reserve, 1800–1801, was alone and on horseback. He faced numerous challenges from the physical landscape and its often crude settlers.

"I find the theatre of action between Zion's King, and the powers of darkness, extends throughout this deep forest. Satan has set up his standard here with variegated colours," he reported to society trustees in a July 27, 1801 letter.

Nevertheless, Badger spoke well of the economic and agricultural potential of this land. When called to return to the Reserve as its resident missionary, Badger agreed but with the stipulation that his wife and six children accompany him and receive support. His hardships started as soon as he attempted to enter the harbor at Ashtabula; a sandbar blocked the entrance, and he had to unload his goods on the bar and cart them to shore.

The additional responsibility of caring for his family in this wilderness—they settled in a log cabin in Austinburg—greatly complicated his work and modified his view of New Connecticut's potential. "If I would have realized and known the difficulties, fatigues & expence [*sic*] of moving my family to this country before I sat [*sic*] out, I should have stayed in New England, or have attempted a shorter remove," he wrote on June 8, 1802, in a letter to the trustees.

The society paid Badger seven dollars per week for his services, an amount totally inadequate to cover the expenses of eight people against the wilderness. The grumpy martyr wrote, "My wife and children severely felt the want of clothing for decency and comfort. Did they expect I would drop my family among the trees, without cover; and enter the field of labour?"

Badger also had to deal with the "bodily exercises," physical manifestations of a spiritual stirring that came with the Second Great Awakening's religious fervor. On November 6, 1803, while preaching to a group of saints in Deacon J. Case's barn in Austinburg, his congregants came under the power.

"Preached twice to a very solemn assembly," he wrote in his diary. "Several were in deep distress, and became unable to support themselves. As the distressed were unable to go from the barn, prayer, exhortation and singing were continued until after the sun was down. As three children, twelve or thirteen years old, were going from the barn to my house they all fell helpless. They were taken up and taken care of. One of them continued in a perfectly helpless situation for more than twelve hours."

The movement resulted in a revival that added forty-one souls to the congregation in Austinburg Township, where Badger organized a Congregational assembly on October 24, 1801.[13]

Above: The unfinished Congregational Church at Austinburg was used for Betsey Cowles's funeral. The church was organized by Reverend Joseph Badger. *Author's collection.*

Right: Betsey Cowles was a teacher, suffragist and abolitionist who devoted her life to improving those of others. She was motivated by the Congregational faith that her father, Giles, preached in Austinburg. *Author's collection.*

"There being a small number of professors in the place were desirous of being instituted into a church, a meeting was appointed for Thursday, October 24, and a church formed, consisting of ten males and six females," he wrote in his journal.

Austinburg and Betsey Cowles

Badger, who traveled throughout the Western Reserve preaching the gospel, was often away from the congregation that he founded. By 1810, the pastoral drought in Austinburg had become so intolerable that Mrs. Eliphalet Austin, wife of the community's namesake settler, saddled up her horse and headed back to New England in search of a full-time pastor.

Her journey back to the Austins' native Connecticut took thirty days. She began her recruitment effort by convincing Sally Cowles, wife of the Congregational preacher she had targeted, that there was both need and opportunity in the Western Reserve.

On May 21, 1811, Reverend Giles Cowles, Sally and their eight children left Bristol, Connecticut, bound for Austin's Camp. He thus became the first settled minister of Austinburg and Morgan Townships, building on the missionary work performed by Badger, who by that time had moved to Ashtabula (his old house still stands). Their furniture and the pastor's precious library were loaded onto two wagons; the pastor, his wife and their two smaller children rode in a carriage.

A year after arriving in the township, Reverend Cowles inspired the congregation to raise a fine meetinghouse, one that was not occupied until 1815 and took another five years to complete. Reverend Cowles also championed education and was a member of the Grand River Presbytery, which established the first Western Reserve college. Cowles also assisted in the work of founding Grand River Institute and was one of the original incorporators.

Revival swept through the Austinburg community in 1831. Among those touched by the stirring was Betsey Cowles, who, twenty years earlier, had made the journey to the Reserve in the arms of her mother. A young, bright woman who was employed as a teacher, Betsey shifted the focus of her life's work from the temporal to the eternal after experiencing that revival.

Four years later, with the death of their father, Betsey and her sisters became eligible for support from the estate Giles left behind. Betsey rejected

The house built by Reverend Giles Cowles still stands in Austinburg Township on Route 45. *Author's collection.*

that offer and felt it necessary to provide her own way in this world. She moved to Oberlin and enrolled in the college's ladies' course to further prepare herself for the task of teaching.

She was a member of the college's third graduating class for women. After graduation, Betsey taught three years at Portsmouth, Ohio, and then returned to Austinburg, where she took charge of the "female department" of the Grand River Institute.

It was during this time that Betsey became friends with antislavery people from Stark County. Infuriated by the stories of mistreatment and bondage, Betsey committed herself to fighting slavery. She served as the secretary of the Ashtabula Female Antislavery Society, which had four hundred members and was one of the largest such groups in Ohio. She also became a disciple of William Lloyd Garrison, prominent American abolitionist and one of the founders of the American Antislavery Society. Garrison, upon Betsey's invitation, visited Ashtabula County and presented his case for immediate emancipation. There were other great abolitionists of the day who visited the county as a result of Betsey's prominence and eloquence, including Stephen S. Foster, Henry C. Wright, Parker Pillsbury, Oliver Johnson, Lucretia Mott and Abby Kelley.

Betsey Cowles requested that the front room of her house be left essentially as it was when she died. Descendants have honored that wish for more than 140 years. *Author's collection.*

In the eyes of many conservative Ashtabula County Christians, however, Betsey Cowles had walked away from her "first love," a commitment to Jesus Christ, and replaced it with an agenda of social reform. Further, Betsey's speeches in the "assembly" were contrary to the Apostle Paul's instructions in I Corinthians 14, that women ought to "keep silence" when the saints assemble for worship. Her boldness thus subjected her to criticism from those in her own camp, as well as those indifferent to the slavery issue.

Betsey's rebuttal can be found in her 1845 address to the antislavery association in Orwell, where she eloquently entreated her audience "by the pure principles of the religion of Jesus Christ…to unite with us in doing all that we can to overthrow a system so vile, so demoralizing, so subversive in the interests and rights of man and of the government of God."

Betsey also adopted the suffrage cause. In 1850, a women's rights convention was held in Salem, Columbiana County. The convention was held in anticipation of a constitutional convention that was to be convened later that year. The attendees elected Betsey as president to preside at the Salem convention, the purpose of which was to provide input regarding women's rights issues to be included in the new Ohio Constitution.

The following year, she attended the Akron Woman's Rights Convention and reported on labor and wages. In 1852, she was named a member of the executive committee of the Ohio Woman's Rights Association.

On the day Lincoln issued his Emancipation Proclamation, Betsey Cowles said, "The two great tasks of my life are ended together: My teaching is done, and the slaves are free."

The faith that set a fire in Betsey's heart during the revival of 1831 was rekindled in her final years. She turned her attention to the task of building a new Congregational church in Austinburg, and it was mainly through her efforts that the brick structure that stands there today was erected. The first public service held within the walls of this church was her funeral.

"So tired; I am so tired," Betsey wrote in her diary three months before her death on July 25, 1876.

METHODISTS AND BAPTISTS

Methodist and Baptist evangelists also cultivated the Reserve's spiritual soil. Methodism, founded by brothers John and Charles Wesley in Great Britain, came to the colonies through missionaries first sent forth in 1769. Theirs was a message of "conversion," of having a "born again" experience and filling of the Holy Spirit.

The message spread like fleas in a kennel. Circuit riders began working the North American frontier in the 1780s. By 1840, the denomination had grown to 580,000 members, the largest in Protestant denomination in the United States.

Reverend Obed Crosby arrived in Trumbull Township in 1805 and established there the first Methodist class in New Connecticut. Competing against Badger in Ashtabula County, it took several years to form a congregation "up north." The first attempt to hold a quarterly meeting of Methodists in Ashtabula was interrupted by news of General William Hull's surrender at Detroit (War of 1812). Nevertheless, the Methodists of Ashtabula date the start of their congregation to those meetings.

The Methodist practice of itinerant circuit riders fit well with the rural nature of Ashtabula County and, in part, explains the large number of small, country Methodist congregations that remain to this day. The godly settlers of Richmond Township were early adopters of the Methodist message. They began meeting under this banner in 1811, but it was not until 1849 that the Methodists had their own building, at Padanarum. Shortly thereafter, the Wesleyan Methodists, a holiness branch of the denomination, built their house of worship. And Richmond United Methodist Church was organized in 1854 as a Methodist Episcopal Church by an English missionary from Africa.

Steamburg had a Methodist church, and Leon had a United Brethren. The latter denomination merged with the Methodist in 1968 to form the "United Methodist" union. Again, this explains why there are so many Methodist congregations in this relatively thinly populated county; it was a case of expansion by acquisition.

Methodists were very busy in Monroe Township, organizing no fewer than three churches: Kelloggsville (1832), Monroe Center (1835) and Clark's Corners (1860). And while the Congregationalists already had a church building in the community when the first Methodist congregation began meeting, only the Methodist presence survived.

The Methodist message also found adherents in the fledgling villages of Ashtabula County. Methodist Episcopal congregations were organized at Jefferson in 1811, Ashtabula and Windsor in 1812, Saybrook in 1816 and Austinburg in 1819. In general, while the rural congregations erected frame buildings, the Methodists of the cities, where there was more wealth and perhaps a greater desire to match the ostentatious buildings of other denominations, used stone and brick when upgrading their buildings.

Baptists came out of English Puritanism in the seventeenth century and were viewed by the Congregationalists and Presbyterians as radically dangerous dissenters who espoused complete separation of church and state. As their name implies, they also, beginning around 1641, insisted on whole-body immersion as a sign of the inward change brought upon them by God's grace. Persecuted in England, the Baptists found religious freedom in New England, where the Rhode Island Yearly Meeting of General Baptists, representing four congregations, was first held in 1670.

The Baptist tradition was as prone to splintering as barn siding; some fifty divisions are known in the United States. One of the points of disagreement was the educational qualifications of pastors and whether sermons ought to be scripted or led by the Spirit. Baptists also divide theologically into Calvinist (Regular Baptists) and Arminian (General Baptists) camps, missionary/anti-missionary sentiments, cultural distinctions and centralized denominational structures.

The strong Puritan influence in New England kept a lid on Baptist fever until the Great Awakening set fire to the souls of men and women from

The first church on the Stanhope-Kelloggsville Road was organized in 1818 in West Andover. The Congregational Church disbanded and donated the building to the trustees. A Southern Baptist congregation remodeled the structure and worships in it. *Author's collection.*

New England to Virginia. Separate Baptists were drawn out of their Puritan roots, and the denomination spread across the new country as its adherents embraced their role as missionaries to the lost.

The first Baptist Association to be organized in Ohio was the Miami, in 1798. Northeast Ohio's Grand River association was formed in 1817 and would include Ashtabula (founded 1825), Jefferson (1811), Geneva (1816), Conneaut (1831) and Kingsville (1813). All of these congregations still exist.

In Conneaut, the Free Will Baptists organized on December 30, 1826. That church continues to this day as South Ridge Baptist, a fundamental Baptist congregation.

Many splinters of the Baptist faith are to be found in Ashtabula County, from the well-established, brick edifices of the "First" churches aligned with the American Baptist Denomination to fundamentalist "Bible Baptist," predominantly black congregations and several Southern Baptist congregations, which started as missionary outreaches to the community in the latter half of the twentieth century. Interestingly, at least one Baptist congregation and a Christian school representing fundamentalist leanings worship and teach in buildings where Congregationalists once worshipped.

Episcopalians

Solomon Griswold, one of the early settlers of what would become Windsor Township, graciously received Congregationalist Joseph Badger into his home. Indeed, the first sermon preached in the township was delivered by Badger in Griswold's home, and there is an account of Griswold's daughters walking sixteen miles round trip through the forest to hear Badger preach in "nearby" Mesopotamia. But Griswold was an Episcopalian, the American offshoot of the Church of England. Thus, in 1816, when the first church in Windsor Township was erected, it was Episcopal. Financed largely with funds from Griswold, it became known as "Solomon's Temple," despite its very rustic nature.

In 1834, a much more stately structure was raised as a meetinghouse for the Episcopalians of the area. However, Christ Church, as it was known, could not complete with the evangelistic fervor of the Methodists and Baptist congregations in the area, and it closed after a few decades. The old structure was rescued by the Ashtabula County Historical Society in the 1950s, and today, it is a museum owned by the Windsor Historical Society.

Christ Church was raised in Windsor Township in 1832, about sixteen years after Solomon's Temple was built to meet the worship needs of the area's Episcopalians. The handsome building is owned by the Windsor Historical Society. *Author's collection.*

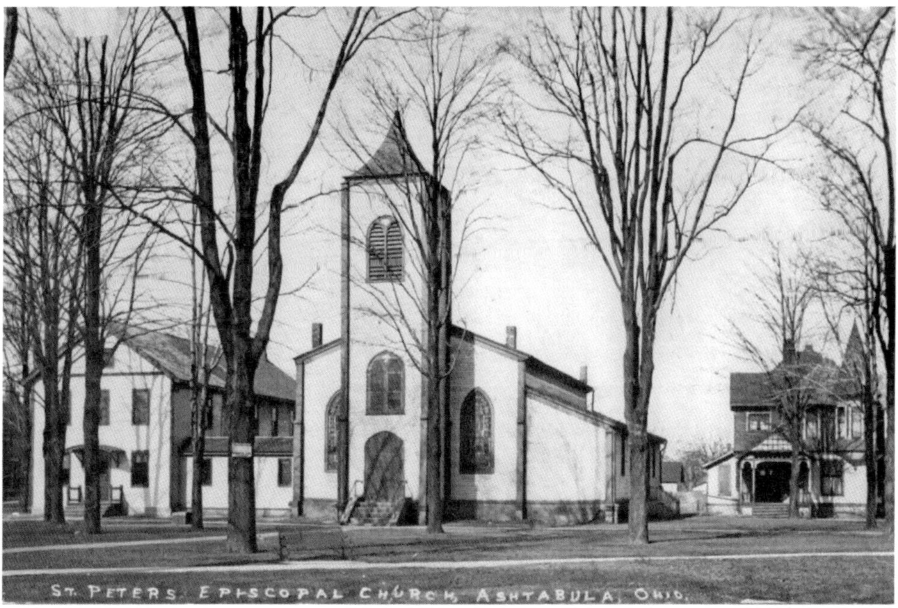

St. Peter's Episcopal Church in Ashtabula was organized on September 26, 1817. The frame building in this photograph was consecrated in 1829; it has since been replaced with a more functional building. *Ashtabula County Historical collection.*

The Episcopalians fared much better in Ashtabula, where Ohio's first parish of that denomination was organized on February 9, 1817. Episcopalian services had been held in Plymouth Township for several years prior. The first families to settle in the township as a unit were those of Zadock Mann. Episcopalians, the Manns opened their cabin to other families of like faith for worship. When their former pastor from New England, Reverend Roger Searle, visited the settlement in 1817, he led the eleven communicants in the formation of a new congregation. Searle named the parish "St. Peter's."

The parish still exists, its tall steeple and clean lines attesting to a denominational heritage born across the ocean and carried westward in the hearts of New England settlers.

SECOND WAVE

The faith of native soil also defined the churches that came with the second wave of religious expansion in the county.

The arrival of the railroads at Ashtabula Harbor in the early 1870s, and at Conneaut later in the century, created a huge need for laborers. Unloading an ore boat was a gritty and difficult job that took days. A typical ore boat would require the labors of 150 men using only shovels and wheelbarrows. A labor shortage soon developed, and immigrants rushed in to fill it.

Faith, kin and traditions defined the enclaves they formed: Roman Catholic churches for the Irish and Italian immigrants and Lutheran for those who came from Finland, Germany and Sweden. Scotch and English immigrants found a home in established Presbyterian, Episcopalian and Methodist congregations.

A small crew of Finnish immigrants, assigned to the job of shoveling at Hanna Docks, arrived in Ashtabula Harbor in 1874. They had saved or borrowed enough to cross the Atlantic and make their way to Northeast Ohio. Frugal and patient, they saved their earnings until there was enough to buy a house and send for the family. At the low rate of pay on the docks, that often took years.

The few became many, and by 1891, there were 1,300 Finland-born residents in Ashtabula alone. They numbered more than 4,000 by 1939.

Russell Holmstrom's grandfather Oscar Ferdinand Holmstrom arrived in Ashtabula Harbor in 1888 at the age of eighteen. He learned carpentry

Ashtabula Harbor led the Great Lakes in tonnage handled at its docks, thanks in part to the labor of immigrants. As mechanization replaced shovels and wheelbarrows, the immigrants found other work as machinery operators, carpenters, business owners and farmers. *Ashtabula County Historical Society collection.*

and built his own house, as well as the parsonage for the first Bethany Lutheran Church.

According to Russell Holmstrom, there were at least five churches in Ashtabula Harbor that catered to the needs of the Finnish. The Finnish Congregational Mission was organized in 1890 and a small house of worship dedicated two years later. The Finnish Evangelical Lutheran, organized in 1890, had grown to 150 members in just three years. A split in the church resulted in the New Finnish Evangelical Lutheran Church, which had 400 members. Both churches had parochial schools.

Bethany Lutheran was formed in 1891 and remains to this day. Reverend Abel Kivioja was the church's first pastor. Just two years after being established, the congregation dedicated its first building. It soon had a Sunday school enrollment of four hundred.

The Finnish immigrants also found community in Sovinto Hall, a social center that offered everything from dances and political programs to roller-skating and an orchestra.

Swedish immigrants settled on the east side of the Ashtabula River, in an area that became known as "Swede Town." The subdivision had its own church, Sweden Congregational (organized in 1880), and a school, the Sweden Summer School, where youngsters learned the language of their

Sovinto Hall in Ashtabula was a huge frame building erected to serve the Finnish population. Bethany Lutheran, another denominational offshoot resulting from immigration, is in the background. *Petros collection.*

parents. The Swedish Lutheran Capernium Church was organized in 1879 by Reverend Otto O. Oleen, who also served the Evangelical Lutheran Church of Ashtabula (Messiah Lutheran).

In Conneaut, Finnish immigrants made their appearance around 1890 and, just five years later, were sufficient in number to form the Conneaut Finnish Lutheran Evangelical Congregation with fifty-eight men. Worship services were held in Finnish until 1956, when English took over with the passing of the founding generation.

Also in Conneaut, Kilpi Hall was constructed as a temperance hall to provide a more wholesome social and recreational alternative to the harbor bars. The hall is home to the Conneaut Community Center for the Arts.

The opportunities were not limited to men of brawn and women content to be homemakers. Alfred Carlson, born in Sweden, immigrated to the United States in 1888 and located in Ashtabula Harbor. He ran a grocery business and was one of the Harbor's most esteemed merchants. His brother Patrick was an engineer on the docks for more than thirty years, and another brother, Otto, settled in Geneva. Their congregation of choice was Swedish Lutheran.

The Swedish Lutheran Capernium Church was built in 1885 at "the head of Bridge Street" to serve Swedish immigrants. The parsonage, right, was added some fifteen years later. Although built for the Swedes, the church stood across the river from Swedetown. *Ashtabula County Historical Society collection.*

Elvira Nystrom was born in Sweden on October 2, 1871, and arrived in the United States at the age of twenty-two. She and her husband, August, had five children; aptly experienced, she opened a maternity hospital in Ashtabula in 1917. In 1924, it was considered "one of the finest of its kind in the country." As with the Carlsons, the Nystroms were members of the Swedish Lutheran Church.

For many of the dock and railroad laborers, their jobs were a means to come full circle, to return to the farming careers they knew across the ocean. In Monroe Township, a group of Finnish dairy farmers established the Toimi Co-op store as a market for their milk. In 1937, they purchased a one-room schoolhouse in the township for use as a community center and, under the spiritual guidance of Reverend Sakari Halkola of the Conneaut Finnish Lutheran Church and Reverend Andrew A. Harju of Ashtabula's Finnish Congregational Church, held church services. The organization lasted about twenty years.

The Roman Catholic tradition in the county dates back to the middle of the nineteenth century, when the seeds were sown for both Mother of Sorrows and St. Joseph's in Ashtabula.

Mother of Sorrows, in Ashtabula Harbor, came about through the urging of Captain James P. Devney, Captain William Downs and James Cahill of the harbor. They petitioned Bishop Horstmann of Cleveland to establish a church in the district. The first Mass was celebrated in 1879 in a room above Cheney's Ship Chandlery and Grocery Store. Most of the one hundred or so persons who attended these masses were immigrants: Irish, German, Hungarian, Portuguese and Italian, the latter group being second only to the Finns as the largest ethnic group in Ashtabula. As their numbers grew, so did the need for a place of worship and clergy.

The imposing stone church in Ashtabula Harbor was dedicated on October 20, 1890. The building is on the National Register of Historic Places.

Immigration drove the formation of two other Roman Catholic congregations in Ashtabula, St. Joseph and Mount Carmel. Sacred Heart, in Rock Creek, was built in 1959–60 on land donated by Hungarian immigrants Joseph and Rose Kujbus. Polish immigrants settled in Sheffield Township were the impetus for St. Andrew's. Geneva's Assumption Church provided a place of worship for the Slovenian immigrants, who were drawn to the county's grape- and fruit-growing region.

MOUNTAIN FAITH

The third wave of religious diversity came between the years 1930 and 1960, when thousands of migrants from the Appalachian Highlands headed north in search of work.

A prior migration from West Virginia to the Western Reserve occurred during the years of America's involvement in World War I, when the rubber factories of Akron tapped Appalachia for workers. Those workers established a beachhead in the industrial Western Reserve that would give their nephews, younger brothers and cousins an inside track on post–World War II job opportunities.

Additionally, in Ashtabula County there was, stretching back to the late 1800s, a small migration of West Virginia natives to the abundant, flat and relatively inexpensive farmland of Ashtabula and Trumbull Counties. J.S. VanCourt, whose family we'll explore in greater depth in the "Unmarked Graves" chapter, was born in a log cabin in West Virginia in 1871. He came to Ohio in 1905 and settled on forty acres in Richmond Township, where he made his mark as a dairy farmer.

The chemical/industrial complex along Lake Road in Ashtabula Township created thousands of jobs and drew migrant workers from the Southern Highlands during the 1940s and '50s. They infused the region with their cultural and religious preferences, such as country music and Pentecostal denominations. *Ashtabula County Historical Society collection.*

During World War II and the two decades thereafter, industry in Ashtabula County grew much faster than the labor force. A major player in this expansion was the government war plant that was built near Lake Erie in Ashtabula Township. The plant produced iron alloys that went into manufacturing heavy equipment used in the war effort. It also produced calcium carbide, an intermediary chemical used in acetylene production. After the war, the huge facility, with its electric furnaces, was converted to peacetime use. Union Carbide Company, which operated the plant during the war years, purchased and expanded the facility. Electrometallurgical Company, or Electro-Met, as the locals referred to it, became a powerhouse industry, employing more than two thousand workers between its various divisions.

Concurrently, producers of chlorinated organic chemicals, titanium sponge, PVC and other chemicals set up shop along the lakeshore. The county's economy boomed, and thousands of migrants from the Southern Highlands, where mechanization had eliminated many of the mainstay mining jobs, headed north. Electro-Met sent recruiters to Kentucky, West Virginia and southern Ohio and paid workers a bonus if they referred a relative or friend to a job in the factory. Some of the recruits quit on the lunch hour of their first day because the work was so dirty, hot and dusty. Others stuck it out and built substantial lives for their families on the above-average wages the industry paid.

Religion was as much a part of these migrants' lives as a passion for the outdoors and kin; faith was the way one could simultaneously reconcile Appalachia's beauty and misery.

While there were Methodist and Baptist congregations in Ashtabula County that offered an approach to the gospel familiar to these migrants, the Holiness, Pentecostal, Church of Christ (non-instrumental) and Old Regular Baptist traditions were missing.[14] Soon, pastors who had served the flocks back home were called to organize and shepherd the migrants in what had become, for the third time, an economic promised land for a disadvantaged but very capable group of people.

One of the larger congregations to come out of this migration is the Ashtabula Revival Center on Cook Road in Ashtabula Township. The church was started by Rose Lee Long, a Kentucky native who grew up in a Baptist church but was always curious about Pentecostalism. Her mother prohibited Rose Lee from attending, but at the invitation of a friend, Rose Lee went to a revival where a Pentecostal pastor was preaching. She ended up marrying the preacher, Raleigh Long, a coal miner who preached as a sideline.

With no work in Kentucky and little cash in preaching, the couple migrated to Cleveland and, in 1956, retired in Ashtabula (Raleigh was considerably older than Rose Lee). Although they worshipped at the Pentecostal Holiness Church, it was not the style of worship to which they were accustomed. Following a failed attempt to start a Church of God, Rose Lee fasted and prayed for the direction her ministry ought to take. At two o'clock one morning, Rose Lee's attention was directed to a block building at West Fifty-seventh Street and Main Avenue. Later that day, she made a deal with the owner for an eighty-dollar-per-month rent, took the money she'd saved for the gas bill at her house and rented the building.

"It was an old, dirty place. I didn't know if I could do it or not, but I knew that if the Lord was in it, I could do it," she told the author in an interview.

The church, a "revival center," grew quickly but had no pastor. James Mullins, a West Virginia native who married Raleigh's daughter, recalled the work of his cousin, Henry Roberts, back in their home state. Roberts was an itinerant Pentecostal evangelist who once described the sensation of the Holy Spirit as "almost like electricity running through your body."

Henry Roberts spent the first decade of his ministry preaching at tent meetings and revival services throughout Appalachia. But in 1961, he reluctantly

Rose Lee Long stands outside the building in downtown Ashtabula where she started the Revival Center. *Author's collection.*

agreed to preach a series of sermons at Rose Lee's revival center. On a return trip/vacation five months later, he was invited to be their pastor, but Roberts wasn't fond of the region. He and his wife, Angie, "put out the fleece"—that is, asked God for a sign. While driving around Ashtabula, a motorist behind them flagged them down, and a woman in the car got out and asked him if he'd like a job. The "fleece" was damp; their future was sealed, but it would not be easy.

There was an overall mistrust and misunderstanding of the Southern Highland migrants, often called "hillbillies" by the northerners. Pentecostalism emphasizes emotional and physical response to the Spirit's presence in worship and can include clapping, speaking in tongues, shouting, dancing and even falling on the floor, giving them the nickname "holy rollers."

Henry and Angie Roberts persevered against these and other odds, fully convinced it was God's will that they be in Ashtabula County and serve the young congregation. The numbers increased each year, and the congregation eventually built a large worship center on the east side of the city. Kenneth Roberts, their youngest son, serves as pastor to the flock of several hundred, most of whom trace their roots to West Virginia or Kentucky.

Similarly, in Geneva Township, the Lily of the Valley Old Regular Baptist Congregation is rooted in the hollows of eastern Kentucky. Founded in

Reverend Henry Roberts and his wife, Angie, followed the leading of the Spirit to Ashtabula, where Henry became pastor to the Revival Center. *Author's collection.*

1966 by Kentucky migrants, the congregation adheres to worship practices dating back hundreds of years and often looking like the Puritanism of the early settlers—sexually segregated seating, only men are allowed to speak in worship, non-instrumental worship and songbooks with lyrics only. The melodies are preserved by oral tradition, and the hymns are lined—that is, a leader sings each line first, and the worshippers repeat it.

DIVERSITY

In a storefront church a couple of miles from Lily of the Valley, a Hispanic congregation raises its hands in spirited worship and a language unintelligible to most other Christians gathered for worship in Ashtabula County. They are the fourth wave, writing a new chapter in the faith history of Ashtabula County, even as the other chapters continue to add footnotes and addendums to their stories. Two themes permeate every chapter—migration/immigration and faith in action. And at no point in Ashtabula County's history did the latter write more history—and attempt to hide it—than during the years leading up to the American Civil War.

3
UNDERGROUND RAILROAD

Thou shalt not deliver unto his master the servant which is escaped from his master unto thee; he shall dwell with thee, even among you, in the place which he shall choose in one of thy gates, where it liketh him best; thou shalt not oppress him.
—Deuteronomy 23:15, 16

Faith without works is dead," declared the writer of the New Testament book of James. In Ashtabula County, the Congregational, Universalist and other social-reform leaning denominations put their Christian faith into action on a fast track of hidden history.

This was a point of pride for those residents who risked fortunes and freedom for the causes of liberty and justice. Many of the residents who adopted this cause were the grandchildren of New Englanders who, a half-century earlier, took up the sword against England in the Revolutionary War. Nonconformity and rebellion, even to the point of treason, were justified if civil law usurped the moral code. These values were grounded in the Christian denominations explored in the prior chapter. In Conneaut, the Free Will Baptists rejected a pastoral candidate because he owned three slaves and refused to grant them liberty. The Conneaut Anti-Slavery Society was formed and hosted numerous speakers who helped transform a political issue into a spiritual one for the congregants. When the Fugitive Slave Law was passed, the South Ridge people declared that they would adhere to the "Bible Fugitive Slave Law," Deuteronomy 23:15, 16, instead.

Antislavery societies proliferated in the county, with the countywide society formed in 1832 and the female countywide society in which Betsey Cowles served coming two years later.

These societies went beyond rhetoric; many of the members also facilitated Underground Railroad (UGRR) operations in the Western Reserve. The UGRR was not a railroad in the sense of an operation with tracks, locomotives and cars but a highly organized system of volunteers who assisted the fugitives in their quest for Canadian soil. The Fugitive Slave Act allowed owners and slave catchers to pursue and retrieve their "property" even in those states, like Ohio, where slavery was not practiced. Therefore, once the fugitive reached the "free states," he or she rode this "underground railroad" to safety.

The railroad had many routes, but the destination was usually Canada because slavery was abolished throughout the British Empire in 1834. Ashtabula County was ideally situated for this clandestine activity. Both Ashtabula and Conneaut offered ports through which these fugitives could stow away on a schooner headed for a Canadian port across Lake Erie. Further, the shortest distance between the slave state of Virginia and Lake Erie lay between the Ohio River in Columbiana County and Ashtabula County's ports. A heavily traveled turnpike, now Route 45, linked the river to the lake. Other north–south roads in the county, including the old Blodgett's Turnpike, flanked by woodlands, barns and the homes of sympathetic residents, were transformed into railroads to freedom.

In Ashtabula Harbor, there still stands the Hubbard House, known as Mother Hubbard's Cupboard to the Underground Railroaders. This was the final stop before boarding one of the schooners headed to Canada, the northern terminus for the Ashtabula County section of this railroad.

The Hubbards were typical of the New England–sourced, abolitionist citizens of Ashtabula County whose Puritan religious background incited them to risk temporal wealth for a greater cause, much as they had done during the American Revolution. "Puritanism mingled with pure patriotism may be said to have constituted the unwritten but inexorable code of moral aggression which the great political battles of the mid-century were fought, and they nowhere had fuller sway than here," wrote Alfred Matthews in "Ohio and Her Western Reserve." "The old-time Puritanical sense of justice and regard for freedom had come by a marvelous stride in human understanding to include justice and freedom for the man who was black as well as for the man who was white."

Nehemiah Hubbard was one of the thirty-nine investors in the Connecticut Land Company. He owned about fifty-eight thousand acres

The Hubbard House, built in 1834, was the home of Colonel William and Katherine Hubbard and served as a terminus of the Underground Railroad. *Author's collection.*

of land in the Western Reserve but was too aged to personally inspect it. Nehemiah instead sent his nephews, William, Matthew and Henry Hubbard, to manage the land and handle sales. William and his wife, Katharine, purchased nearly fifty acres of this real estate and, in the early 1840s, built a house near the shore of Lake Erie in what would become Ashtabula City.

Matthew, Henry and William were members of the Ashtabula County Anti Slavery Society. They were more than members in name; the Hubbards, particularly William and Katharine, risked their wealth by disobeying the Fugitive Slave Act and hiding runaway slaves in their home and the Hubbard family warehouse on the Ashtabula River. While no written records of their activity were kept, an eyewitness claimed to have seen 39 slaves hiding under the Hubbards' protection, or "39 slaves made short work of a barrel of pickles," referring to the fugitives' appetite.

Getting this human cargo to Mother Hubbard's Cupboard required the work of dozens of conductors throughout the county. According to the Hubbard House Underground Railroad Museum's research, the county had more than thirty UGRR stations, or safe houses, and many more conductors who lived in Ashtabula, Austinburg, Rome, Cherry Valley,

This house on Stanhope-Kelloggsville Road was a station on the Underground Railroad. Known as the Carpenter House, it had a secret hiding place under the second-story room on the front of the house. *Ashtabula County Historical Society collection.*

Conneaut, Richmond Center, Jefferson, Andover, Lindenville, West Andover and West Williamsfield.

Our familiar byway, Stanhope-Kelloggsville Road, had several safe havens, including one that was said to have been built specifically for the purpose of harboring fugitives. Leverett Osburn was a carpenter who designed and built the house in 1842–43. Standing about a mile north of West Andover, Osburn's creation was known as "the tower house." Dwight (in some sources "Jahaziel") Carpenter was the next owner, and it was known as the "Carpenter House" during the Civil War. By 1932, it was being referred to as the "Gray Farm."

This house no longer stands, but its function was understood by its abolitionist builder, owners and neighbors in those antebellum days. And its prewar history came to light with a knock on the door years after the nation's reunification.

The owner, who had acquired it after the UGRR was no longer necessary, found standing there an elderly black man named Edward Howard, a former slave, who had followed the drinking gourd north to his freedom in Canada. Back in the United States, he was traveling the old State Road and requested the owner's permission to tie up his horse on the land and sleep in his wagon. The owner granted the request and offered a portion of his dinner to him. The man humbly accepted the offer and ate the meal alone, on the seat of his wagon.

The next morning, Howard asked permission to look inside the house, for he related a story about how he had spent two or three days and nights there, hiding from the slave catchers. A neighbor was visiting the family and corroborated the events that followed. The old man, climbing the steps, pulled out a section of the stairway and pointed to hiding place of which the owners had no knowledge. The space was beneath the "captain's lookout" and occupied an area three feet above the first-floor ceiling. The hiding place tapered off under the eaves of the house. The space was sufficient to conceal a dozen men, and bedding was still in place from those UGRR adventures.

A trapdoor and a shaft, disguised as a chimney, provided a passageway into the cellar.

The man shared his story of spending very tense moments in the hiding place and hearing the stomping of the slave catchers on the steps as they climbed to the lookout, where ladies were engaged in a quilting party. He also told how the nearby blacksmith used his anvil to warn neighbors of an approaching slave catcher. The blacksmith repeated a specific number of blows to the anvil to sound the alarm.

The Carpenter House was razed a number of years ago, but another house associated with Osburn and the UGRR still stands to the south, at West Andover. The Greek Revival home on Stanhope-Kelloggsville Road is credited to Osburn's hammer and labor.[15] It is known as the House of 10,000 Spools, a reference to myriad wooden "spool" ornaments that are used as decorative elements. Its construction date was between 1845 and 1850.

While lacking the anecdotal evidence of being a railroad stop, during restoration an eighteen-inch space between the floors was discovered. This space connected the house's three attic spaces, suggesting a place for hiding humans and providing an escape route.

Another Stanhope-Kelloggsville house that was associated with the UGRR stood on the west side, south of West Andover. It was known as the "Coleman Place."

Moving passengers from station to station was often done at night to evade the slave owners and catchers who frequently were on their trail. Some clever abolitionists had wagons with false bottoms, under which a

The House of 10,0000 Spools stands on Stanhope-Kelloggsville Road, just north of Route 6 in West Andover. Also known as the Byron Bishop home, it is of Grecian design and was associated with the Underground Railroad. *Author's collection.*

The Lyman Peck home on Route 46 is one of Ashtabula County's octagonal homes and was a stop on the Underground Railroad. *Author's collection.*

fugitive or two could be hidden and transported northward. Such was the modus operandi of Lyman Peck of New Lyme, who made many late-night trips with his wagon from the family's octagonal home.

The odds were against a slave catcher or owner who attempted to recover his property from Ashtabula County, even though financial incentives were available to residents who provided information that led to capture. One discouraged slaveholder observed that it "was easier to get a saint out of hell than a slave out of Austinburg (Township)." Indeed, no fugitive slave was ever recovered from any place in Ashtabula County.

THE JOHN BROWN CONNECTION

Ashtabula County's antislavery sentiment was heard all the way in the U.S. House, although the proslavery block tried repeatedly to silence the voice of Representative Joshua R. Giddings (1795–1864). Born in Bradford County, Pennsylvania, Giddings moved to Ashtabula County with his parents in 1806. The family's farm was located in Wayne Township, near Stanhope-Kelloggsville Road. Giddings served in the War of 1812, worked as a teacher and studied law with Elisha Whittlesey. Admitted to the bar in 1821, Giddings developed a reputation as an excellent lawyer and became quite wealthy. From 1831 to 1837, he was in partnership with Benjamin Wade, who shared Giddings's distaste for slavery, became a U.S. senator and came within one impeachment vote of becoming president.

Joshua Giddings was a fiery abolitionist congressman from Ashtabula County. He was censured by his peers, but the voters of the county sent him back to the House, where he served in the decades leading up to the Civil War. *Library of Congress collection.*

The law office in which Joshua Giddings practiced still stands in Jefferson. This image shows the office as it appeared in the 1930s. *Library of Congress collection.*

Giddings served one term in the Ohio House; after the Panic of 1837, in which he lost much of the fortune he had accumulated from his law practice, Giddings went into national politics. From December 1838 until March 1859, Giddings represented Ashtabula County's predominately abolitionist sentiment.[16] A physically intimidating man with an intellect and verbal delivery to match, Giddings worked tirelessly to abolish slavery and predicted that only military action would settle the dispute. He backed his rhetoric with action, providing respite for runaways in his Jefferson office and home. There is documentation that both Giddings and Wade gave cash toward the purchase of a fugitive slave's freedom. And in May 1859, when John Brown came to Ashtabula County to raise money for his abolitionist activities, Giddings met with Brown in the little law office that still stands at the county seat.[17]

That summer, a dozen or so of the twenty-one men involved in John Brown's raid on the federal arsenal at Harpers Ferry, Virginia, lived and worked on farms in the southeastern section of Ashtabula County as they awaited their marching orders from the Kennedy farmhouse in Maryland near Harpers Ferry. There is no evidence that the people of the county with connections to Brown were aware of his plan to raid the arsenal, arm the slaves of nearby plantations and begin the bloody fight to end slavery. Nor were the antislavery sentiments so strong in Ashtabula County that the populace would have approved of this bold strike of treason. Indeed, there was agitation among the folks of the county when news of the raid reached the community—who knew what kind of documentation the federal investigators would find among Brown's correspondence? He had been to Ashtabula County just five months earlier, and there were several dozen souls with county addresses who had connections to Brown.

During the summer of 1859, at West Andover, letters were sent to Brown and his son, John Jr., in care of Horace Lindsley, whose dwelling was on the west side of Stanhope-Kelloggsville Road and doubled as an UGRR station. The letters were addressed to "I. Smith & Son" and provided updates on the visionary's efforts to accumulate weapons and recruit men for his bold strike. Aaron V. Stevens, wounded in the raid and hanged for his deeds, also lived with Lindsley.

Other raid participants who spent that summer in southeast Ashtabula County were Edwin Coppic, Oliver Brown, Watson Brown, Albert Hazlett, Stuart Taylor, William Thompson, Adolph Thompson, John H. Kagy, Jeremiah Anderson and John E. Cook.

There were several African American men involved in the raid, and they, too, were connected to Northeast Ohio. Dangerfield P. Newby, Louis Leary, Green Shields, O.P. Anderson and John A. Copeland were in the county during the summer of 1859. Newby worked in a blacksmith shop at Dorset and stayed with Smith Edwards. A former slave who had escaped from a Virginia plantation, Newby's participation in Brown's raid was

Abolitionist John Brown Sr. was a frequent visitor to Ashtabula County. *Library of Congress collection.*

driven by his desire to gain his family's freedom. He felt that overthrowing the federal arsenal at Harpers Ferry would be the first step in that effort.

And then there was the matter of the weapons used in the raid, damning evidence for certain residents of Ashtabula County. In the winter of 1858, there arrived at Ashtabula via rail a shipment of unmarked freight in coffin boxes. Loaded onto bobsleds, this cargo was transported to Jefferson and then Cherry Valley Township, where it was stored in the cabinet shop of King & Brothers.

It later came to light that those boxes contained Sharps carbines, spears and other weapons destined for the insurrection. During their time in Ashtabula County, these boxes were moved from cabinet shop to maple sugar house to barns. In late July 1859, children playing in the haymow of Alex Fobes's barn in Wayne Township discovered the weapons and reported them to adults. Shortly thereafter, the weapons were removed from that barn and taken by wagons to Hartstown, Crawford County, Pennsylvania. The boxes were marked "hardware and castings."

The next day, John Smith (Brown Jr.) wrote a letter to J. Henrie with the following message for "Esquire Smith" (his father): "I yesterday forwarded to canal at Hartstown, Pennsylvania, eleven boxes 'hardware and castings' from King Brothers. They are numbered and marked thus: X1 to 11…X8 and X9 are those which were on store with E.A. F[obes] at Lindenville [Wayne Township]…Write often, directing to John Smith, under cover to Horace Lindsley, as before. Let me know if those goods come through safely. Please say to Mr. S.—— I am ready to serve."

The evidence, it seemed, was stacked against Ashtabula County, whose antislavery congressman refused to stop ranting against the institution of

Weapons for John Brown's raid on Harpers Ferry were hidden in the haymow of this barn in Wayne Township. The structure no longer stands. *Author's collection.*

slavery, whose churches had taken up the cause and whose citizens were involved in breaking the law by aiding escaped slaves and, from evidence that could surface at any moment, appeared to have assisted and financially supported the insurrectionists.

John Brown Sr., seriously wounded in the battle and held in prison, was questioned by a Mr. Vallindingham, a proslavery representative from Ohio. The questioning attempted to link Brown to Giddings and his district, but Brown would say only that his sympathizers were located in "all the free states." Nevertheless, Giddings was summoned after the raid to appear before a congressional committee investigating the incident; at that point, the federal government was concerned that another invasion of Virginia was being developed or, at the very least, that Brown's sympathizers would attempt to raid the Jefferson County, Virginia prison where Brown and four others from the failed raid were being held.

When Brown Jr. and James Redpath of Massachusetts failed/refused to cooperate with a Senate investigation into the raid, warrants for their arrests were issued. An armed marshal was sent across the Ohio River toward Ashtabula County to capture the subjects of interest. He was met by vigilantes from Lenox Township.

John Brown Sr. and a few of his men secured themselves in the engine house at Harpers Ferry after the raid on the arsenal failed. The building was stormed by U.S. Marines led by Colonel Robert E. Lee. *Author's collection.*

"As soon as it was known in Jefferson what the marshal was there for… the boys at once made preparations for a fight. Rifles were brought out and cleaned, bullets were moulded, long knives, which had been made for some by Daniel Williams, the blacksmith, were buckled about the waist or slipped into the bootleg ready for use if needed," wrote Moses Worthington Beede in a memoir of the Black Strings.[18] "That they would be needed was confidently expected and a squad fully armed hurried to Dorset in Brown's defense."

The Senate investigation into the raid stated, "It appeared by the return of the marshal for northern district of Ohio, as deputy sergeant-at-arms, that John Brown Jr., at first evaded the process of the Senate, and afterwards, with a number of other persons, armed themselves to prevent his arrest. The marshal further reported that Brown could not be arrested unless he was authorized in like manner to employ force." Only one Ashtabula County resident, a Mr. S. Dann, offered his assistance to the marshal. Curiously, Dann was interred in a crypt at Oakdale Cemetery, but only the foundation of that building survived; an old gravestone, placed on the rectangular foundation, marks his burial.

The "arming" mentioned in the marshal's report was a reference to the Black Strings, a secret organization that appears to have grown out of the "Committee of 100," a group organized by Giddings in early 1859. The group's purpose was to travel to Cleveland and join other like-minded persons in protesting the jailing of men arrested for aiding a runaway slave, an incident known as the Wellington-Oberlin affair. Among those arrested for breaking federal and state fugitive slave laws was Ralph Plumb, a lawyer with connections to Cherry Valley Township in Ashtabula County. The rally ultimately drew two thousand persons from Ashtabula County alone, at a time when the total population of the county was around thirty-one thousand persons. Although the rally was inconsequential, for Ashtabula County, it was a magnet that drew antislavery iron from the haystacks and galvanized it into action after the Harpers Ferry incident.

The consort thus extracted became the Black Strings—members wore a black string through their shirts' button holes. The group was organized at West Andover by Benjamin Perry, in whose home John Brown had spent his last night in Ashtabula County. An oft-told story has one of the Black Strings standing guard at their first meeting with a pistol that had been given to George Washington by Marquis de Lafayette. J.E. Cook, a leader of the insurrection, allegedly stole the flintlock pistol from the home of Colonel Lewis W. Washington of Harpers Ferry during the raid. Thinking he was doing a favor to Perry, Cook forwarded the firearm to the Black Strings group. Perry, upon learning the story behind the gun, returned it to Washington.[19]

The Black Strings also protected those members of the raiding party who managed to escape and return to Ashtabula County. They were Owen Brown, Barclay Coppic,[20] O.P. Anderson, Francis Merriam and James Redpath.

Black Strings were not simply protecting Brown Jr. and other Harpers Ferry escapees who found their way back to the county; there was plenty of incriminating evidence in the Kennedy farmhouse where Brown's letters and plans were discovered by federal marshals. The Black Strings were looking to protect one another, as well, from interrogation and charges of aiding and abetting a conspiracy. Each Black Strings member took an oath to "protect with his property and his life any person a refugee from Harpers Ferry, or any person in Ashtabula County suspected of complicity, or wanted by the federal government or the state of Virginia as an accomplice of John Brown, or as a witness in the cases on trial at Charlestown, Virginia."

The society was successful in its mission. As Beede noted in his memoir, Brown was moved to the second story of a house on present-day Route 307 in Dorset Township, and armed Black String members were posted outside during the marshal's visit. It is said that the interior walls of the room in which Brown was secured were covered with steel plates. Brown Jr. also hid in the loft over the *Ashtabula County Sentinel* office on Chestnut Street in Jefferson while agents searched for him. In Austinburg, Brown found refuge in the attic of the Cowles home. The pastor's family concealed the door to the attic by pasting wallpaper over it.

Conveniently, the tactics thus used by the Black Strings to protect the anarchist from the government were developed and honed for years in the course of protecting the UGRR passengers.

OPENING SHOTS

It was the opinion of both John Brown Sr. and Joshua Giddings that the slavery issue would be settled only by bloodshed. Given that both prophets had Ashtabula County connections, it was fitting that soldiers from this county were at the first land battle, some say "skirmish," of that era of bloodshed and there had the honor of making the Union's first light artillery attack.

In the days following the Confederate attack on Fort Sumter, Lincoln called on state militia groups to muster and protect strategic locations, including Marietta, Ohio, on the Ohio River.

Among the groups called was the Cleveland Light Artillery, a group of six companies, five in Cuyahoga County and one in Geneva. Cleveland Light Artillery reported to Columbus on the evening of April 22, 1861.

Organized in 1837, the group had just nine men, many of them from the leading families of Cleveland. Perhaps they just wanted a little adventure in their lives or enjoyed playing around with artillery—the state did not recognize the group as militia, and the men had to furnish their uniforms and artillery. They found a six-pound cannon, built a carriage and caisson for it and even made their own ammunition.

Originally part of the Cleveland Grays, the Light Artillery detached from the Grays in 1845. Drill sergeant David Wood was elected captain. Their function was largely ceremonial and to encourage men in other cities to form a light artillery.

By 1851, the state was providing guns to the groups—one gun to a company. A year later, the Cleveland Light proved its value by suppressing a riot at a medical school in Cleveland. In 1859, the state's militia law was changed, and light artillery groups were permitted to muster.

The following year, Geneva, a village in the western corner of the Ashtabula County, formed its light artillery. The unit acquired a brass cannon and drilled with the piece. The Geneva Light, Company F of the First Regiment of Ohio Light Artillery, was commanded by Captain Dennis Kenny. There were twenty-three men under his command.

When Lincoln called on state militia groups to muster, the Cleveland Light marched off to war. After providing security at Marietta, the light artillery was called into western Virginia. There were key bridges in that region, including the one at Fairmont over the Monongahela River and a long covered bridge at Philippi over the Tygart. It was essential to have those bridges remain under Union control. Further, the Union needed to ensure control of the Baltimore and Ohio Railroad, whose western Virginia route ran from Grafton to Wheeling.

The artillery came under the command of Major General George B. McClellan, who planned to occupy the pro-Union western area of Virginia and keep the railroad supply line open. Ultimately, he wanted to beat the Confederate forces all the way back to Richmond.

On May 30, the company left Camp Putnam in Marietta for Grafton. It traveled by steamboat and then train, its guns on a flat car in front of the engine "shotted and ready to repel any attack that might be made," according to the Williams brothers' *History of Ashtabula County*.

A two-column attack was planned on the Confederates camped at Philippi. The Geneva men were part of the column that would march north from Webster, four miles away, along the turnpike. The march commenced at 11:00 p.m. the night prior and continued through drenching rain.

"All night, through the darkness and drenching rain, the two columns pushed on, over roads so rough and muddy that they were in some places almost impassable to artillery. It was only by the aid of the men who swarmed around the carriages and put their hands to the wheels, that the panting horses were able to drag guns and caissons," wrote the unit's historian in *Reminisces of the Cleveland Light Artillery*. "To the volunteers, that night was a baptism indeed. They tried bravely to keep up their spirits as they trudged along through mud and water and stumbled over the roots and stumps and stones that lay in their pathway. It was so dark that a man could scarcely see his file leader. That nocturnal experience knocked the poetry and romance out of 'soldiering' with a suddenness and completeness that was paralyzing."

Some of the men fainted from exhaustion and were left behind; others cast off their haversacks and provisions so they could keep up with the stronger soldiers.

There were 1,600 Union soldiers between the two columns. The start of the predawn attack was to be signaled by a gunshot. Because of the heavy rain, the Confederates had retreated to their tents for the night and did not establish a picket. When a Confederate-sympathizing woman saw the Union soldiers approaching the town, she sent her son on horseback to warn the Southerners. The Union pickets captured him; his mother witnessed the action and shot her pistol at the soldiers. The invading forces took that as a signal to begin the attack, starting with the artillery.

This is where Ashtabula County history was made—the first shot of that battle, the first planned land battle of the Civil War, came from Company F's brass cannon.

"The attack upon the Confederate camp at Philippi was made by this company, and the first shotted gun, after the attack at Fort Sumter, fired in the war was the old brass piece from Geneva, Ashtabula County," states the Williams brothers' book.

Reminiscences of the Cleveland Light Artillery makes no note of this, however. It simply states that "the men had an opportunity to use their guns and they made the most of it, to the extent of sixteen rounds."

Union soldiers from the Cleveland Light Artillery fought at the "Philippi Races" in Philippi, West Virginia, the first land battle/skirmish of the Civil War. The covered bridge was a strategic point in that skirmish, a solid Union victory. *Author's collection.*

The Confederates awoke to the sound of this artillery and many of them fled the scene, still in their nightclothes. Journalists called it the "Philippi Races."

There were at least three serious casualties. Colonel Benjamin Kelley of the Union First Virginia Infantry was shot while pursuing escaping Confederates. Also shot were two Confederate soldiers whose injuries required amputation. They would be the first of thousands to lose limbs in the war.

One of them was James E. Hanger, only eighteen years old and a college student. *Reminiscences of the Cleveland Light Artillery* goes so far as to give credit to the weapons of that group for inflicting the injury. Hanger returned to Virginia and made an artificial leg for himself. The ingenious inventor used barrel staves and hinged the leg at the "knee." The Virginia state legislature liked the design and commissioned Hanger to make these limbs for other maimed soldiers. Thus did the Hanger Orthopedic Group, Inc., get started. According to online sources, as of 2007, it was the United States' leading manufacturer of artificial limbs.

Back in Cleveland, newspapers were praising the men of the Light Artillery as heroes. Given the performance of the Confederates at Phillipi, and the endurance of the Union soldiers, it seemed likely the war would be only a series of skirmishes.

"Indeed, it rather looked as though it was the Southern soldiers who would not fight, and some people believed, after Philippi, that the war was about over. Some of the victorious blue-coats thought so and they felt an exceeding great joy that they had been permitted to participate in the action that was the death-blow to the rebellion," states *Reminiscences of the Cleveland Light Artillery*.

The men of the Geneva Artillery completed their ninety-day commitment and were mustered out in July 1861 at Columbus. But they were soon back in the action as the Fourteenth Ohio Independent Battery. This group, recruited from Ashtabula and surrounding counties, became known as Burrows' Battery, after its captain, Jerome D. Burrows, a Geneva attorney at the time.

He had joined the Geneva Artillery in April 1861 but, according to the roster, did not participate in that group's exploits in western Virginia. Nevertheless, a biography of Burrows published by the Ohio State Bar Association makes the claim that "it was [Burrows's] honor to fire the first cannon on the Union side, in the field after war had been declared."

Geneva's artillery became part of the Fourteenth's arsenal of weapons as that group was mustered into service at Cleveland on September 20,

1861. Most of the men came from Ashtabula, Lake, Trumbull and Geauga Counties. Their commitment was for three years.

The battery was eventually sent to Tennessee in the spring of 1862 and fought at the Battle of Shiloh, April 3 and 4, 1862. The men went into battle with six guns and had to leave all of them behind after suffering heavy losses in the ranks: four men dead and twenty-six wounded, including Burrows, who was hit in the arm. Seventy of their horses were killed.

The battery did not fight the second day, but it did manage to recover its cannons. Perhaps Ashtabula County's brass relic was among them.

Burrows' Battery fared better in subsequent attacks. It was in camp at Lynnville, Tennessee, from June 1863 to March 1864. It was at the Battle of Resaca, Georgia, where it sent 342 rounds of ammunition toward the enemy and did not lose one man in the effort.

At Atlanta, three of the battery's soldiers were killed and eighteen wounded. The battery pounded Atlanta with 651 rounds. After a new supply of horses and harness was drawn at Nashville, the battery was constituted as horse artillery and participated in the pursuit of Hood's demoralized army.

The battery's roster shows that at least six of the men died. Many more were discharged due to illness or disability. Albert E. Griffin lost his arm. S.W and C.R. Waters were discharged for disability on August 26, 1862.

Burrows resigned on August 26, 1864. His arm, shattered at Shiloh, would remain in a weakened condition for the rest of his life. Despite the disability, Burrows lived a very full and productive life, serving as Lake County's prosecuting attorney, a state senator, mayor of Painesville and a circuit court judge.

"He was genial in disposition, lovable in his nature and warm in his affections," his biographer wrote.

4

Mounds, Graveyards and Reverend Spalding

A sure way to confound a future generation is to bury something that is likely to be found without explanation of its purpose, origin or circumstances of demise.

It would appear that a race of giants did just that before the settlers from New England pushed into the Western Reserve to examine their promised land. Many old newspapers and county history books contain stories of a giant race of people who lived on this continent for centuries before Columbus arrived. The skeletal evidence and discovery of metals, inscriptions and implements left behind suggest Columbus simply "rediscovered" what had previously been found but not reported back to the homeland.

These cemeteries, artifacts and skeletons are not to be confused with the burial mounds, fortifications and remains of villages inhabited by indigenous people. Many of these mounds and artifacts associated with indigenous cultures were found in Ashtabula County by pioneers. Indeed, Native Americans continued to hunt and camp in this area until after the War of 1812. The mound-builder cultures do not explain, however, the rectangular burial grounds, orchards, gigantic skeletons, inscriptions and other discoveries that suggest a race familiar with Christian burial practices.

MOUNDS AND ANCIENT CEMETERIES OF ASHTABULA COUNTY

As Described by Early Settlers (Williams Brothers' 1878 History of Ashtabula County*)*

Fort Hill, Conneaut	Conneaut's Fort Hill rises above the Conneaut Creek Valley south of town, just west of State Route 7. This fortification was a natural feature about seventy-five feet high with a man-made but simple earth wall on the edge of the bluff. "The land thus enclosed was perfectly level, and embraced an area of about two acres, triangular in shape." The site is on private property.
Indian Fort, Windsor	A "tongue of land" at the junction of two streams, Phelps and Grindstone Creeks. The land rises abruptly here to a height of one hundred feet. There were two walls, partly constructed of earth, partly of flat stones, parallel to each other, about ten feet apart. Located in Camp Whitewood, the site is on the National Register of Historic Places.
Pymatuning Creek area	Located on a three-acre island, the work of defense was about an acre and a half in size. An eyewitness reported it to the Smithsonian Institution, which published it in a report of 1876. The walled site had an outer wall 5.0 feet tall and an inner 2.5 feet high. Interior width was 250.0 feet and length 300.0 feet. Remains of logs were found in the stream, suggesting a prior stockade.
Wayne Township works	Joel Blakeslee, an early pioneer and historian, described the "ruins of two large excavations, the largest found in the county" near a "fine spring of water called Cold spring." "Rubbish, logs and dirt" were found in the mounds, eighteen to twenty feet wide and seven to eight feet deep. A "grand avenue or royal highway" ran from the mounds to the stream. Farmers found many ancient relics in this area.
Ashtabula City side of the Ashtabula River, behind St. Joseph's Catholic Church	Reverend John Hall, a rector of St. Peter's Episcopal Church, described a beautiful and fertile spot of ground that appeared to be a bit of Eden preserved. "It was the most beautiful and lovely I ever beheld," declared Matthew Hubbard, who first saw it in 1804. The plat yielded many relics, such as pottery fragments, arrowheads, pipes and even stone doorsteps, as the settlers disturbed it for a garden.

Edgewood Cemetery area	Graves of a former people were evident by the sinks or hollows in the soil. Nearly one thousand of these were discovered in regular rows close together. Bones were exhumed that "seemed to have belonged to a race of giants."
Plum Point	On the west bank of the Ashtabula River, near its exit at Lake Erie, a massive mound or burial heap thirty-five feet in diameter and seven feet high was discovered. This mound was destroyed in the 1870s to accommodate lake vessels on the upper end of the river at Ashtabula Harbor.
Near Chestnut Cemetery	A double fortress at the junction of three streams, south of the village and near Chestnut Grove Cemetery, "these two fortifications seemed to answer to one another across the deep gorge."
Saybrook Township	"A beautiful bank with an elevation of about 10 feet, which embraces an area of about one-fourth of an acre, which once contained in regular form 30 or 40 circular sinks or impressions, 2 to 3 feet deep. These were possibly cellars or grain stores. A pipe was found at this location and was finely carved with a figure emblematical of some imaginary being, part man, part beast."
Conneaut	Henry Howe's *Historical Collections of Ohio* recognizes mounds in the eastern part of Conneaut Village and an "extensive burying-ground near the Presbyterian church which appear to have had no connection with the burying-places of the Indians. Among the human bones found in the mounds were some belonging to men of gigantic structure." The four-acre site had some two to three thousand graves in straight rows; upon exposure to air, the blackened bones "soon crumbled to dust." In another reference, Howe reports that a skull and a silver false tooth were discovered in a mound that was cut through while building Harbor Street. The tooth fit perfectly into the jaw of the skull.

One such burial ground was discovered by the early settlers of Salem, the name by which Conneaut City was originally known. Henry Howe, in his *Historical Collections of Ohio*, distinguishes between the burying places of Indians in mounds on the eastern side of the village and an "extensive burying-ground" that was in the village. The latter surrendered bones that were supposed to belong "to men of gigantic structure." "Some of the skulls were of sufficient capacity to admit the head of an ordinary man, and jaw bones that might have been fitted on over the face with equal facility; the other bones were proportionately large," wrote Howe in his Ashtabula County chapter of the Collections.

Further, Howe records a number of points about this burial ground, which was discovered in 1800, that suggest the presence of an advanced culture:

- It contained about four acres and was rectangular in shape, except where the natural contour of the earth dictated a diversion.
- The burial lots appeared to run north and south, and there were slight depressions at each grave; the number of graves was estimated between one and two thousand.
- The ground was covered with "ordinary forest trees," but there was an opening near the center of the burying ground where a single butternut tree was planted.
- Bones recovered from the graves were "blackened by time" and "crumbled to dust" shortly after being exposed to air. One must assume this is why none of these artifacts survive for us to study today.

Howe's entry also points out the presence of squares and terraces laid out into gardens but reclaimed by the forest.

To the west of Conneaut, on the east side of the Ashtabula River, another ancient burial ground, along with a partly buried marker with an inscription, was discovered by the settlers.

The "stone plate or slab" was discovered by the son of Peleg Sweet, an early settler who owned the land on the east side of the Ashtabula River in Ashtabula Township. It is described in great detail in the Williams brothers' *History of Ashtabula County*:

> *It consisted of a stone plate or slab on which were inscribed certain letters. A small tree had been turned up by the roots, near the banks, and this remarkable stone was found sticking into the bank near the top, its end inclining somewhat downwards toward the creek. The stone was taken out of its place, and was seen by a number of citizens, but was neglected, and has been since destroyed or covered up by the washings of the bank. It was, when found, lying with its smooth face downwards, the other side being flat but unpolished. On turning it over it was discovered that its surface was covered with marks of inscribed letters. The lower end seemed to have been*

Edgewood Cemetery in Ashtabula Township occupies mysterious burial grounds, where settlers recorded finding skeletons of a race of giants. *Author's collection.*

> *broken off, but what there was in an oblong shape, twenty-two inches long, fourteen broad, and three inches thick. The top and edges were squarely finished and straight. The inscription was as follows: across the face of the stone, about six inches from the top, were two parallel straight lines cut skillfully (on a bevel), and beneath the lines on the left hand were two Roman capital letters,—"E.P.,"—neatly cut. Beneath this, and about three inches below the lines, was another inscribed line, and beneath the line on the right side two more letters,—"O.S.,"—of similar size and shape. Beneath this again, and three inches below the last mentioned line, were two more lines, and under these, at the left hand again, these figures—"121"—cut in large and distinct outlines, and underneath the figures was still another line, equally distant from the others. From this to the broken edge there was no inscription, and no other marks were found on the stone.*

Despite the great pains that were taken to make measurements, note the inscriptions and record the same, the relic itself was neglected and left on the bank "to perish." Was this a headstone to an unmarked grave or perhaps a memorial to a lost colony that met its demise at this spot along the Ashtabula River?

Fort Hill stood on the lakeshore at Ashtabula before dock expansion required its removal. During the War of 1812, a passing British ship fired at the shoreline, and residents marched around the hill with pitchforks and old guns in an attempt to convince the "invaders" that their forces were robust. Settlers found Indian artifacts in these mounds. *Petros collection.*

Adding to the mystery was the discovery of two human skeletons, face down in the stream's bank, with muskets in their hands. Found near the spot where the river entered Lake Erie, one skeleton's fingers were still clasped about the rusty gun barrel when the grisly discovery was made. There are several possible explanations, including one that we'll explore in the "Unmarked Graves" chapter, which suggests the men were Spanish. Another possibility is that they were French explorers from La Salle's lost *Le Griffon*.[21]

The settlers of Ashtabula village often encountered evidence of prior, ancient peoples who had not only occupied this land but also thrived on it. Reverend John Hall, former rector of St. Peter's Episcopal Church, wrote about these places in his early history of Ashtabula. He stated that, in the rear of the place where St. Joseph's Catholic Church stands, there was a plat of ground where the vegetation was entirely different from that in the surrounding region.

The settlers used this spot as a garden, and Hall observed that it was a favorite haunt of Reverend Badger, whose home was nearby, and of Matthew Hubbard, who, in 1804, declared it the "most beautiful and lovely spot I ever beheld." Consisting of seven or eight acres, the land often yielded arrowheads, pipes and even stone doorsteps, worn smooth by long use. Hubbard noted that while the soil surrounding this "Paradise" was yellow clay, inside the refuge, the dirt was "the most beautiful and yielding imaginable, with a level surface as smooth as a palace walk."

Growing in this soil were black walnut, cherry and mulberry trees with no underbrush. The entire plat was covered with a rich carpet of fine grass.

Across the Ashtabula River gulf, a bit farther upstream on land now the Edgewood Cemetery, was an ancient cemetery with nearly one thousand sinks or hollows in regular rows, close together.

"In cultivating the soil in the vicinity implements have been found, and in excavating the ground for graves it is said bones have been exhumed which seemed to have belonged to a race of giants." Peleg Sweet owned this land, and he told stories of excavating "a skull and jaw which were of such size that the skull would cover his head and the jaw could be easily slipped over his face, as though the head of a giant were enveloping his."[22]

BURIED ROLLS OF PARCHMENT

Pioneers had no explanation for these findings; even the Native Americans who were still among them in those early days could not shed light on the culture of the giants. The mounds, ancient fortifications and graves suggesting "Christian burial" became matches to ignite the imagination and, some would say, an entire religion.

The story begins with Solomon Spalding,[23] Revolutionary War soldier, minister, businessman and graduate of Dartmouth College. His widow, Matilda, writing in a Boston newspaper in May 1839, described him as "distinguished for a lively imagination and great fondness for history." He also was well versed in the Old Testament and classical writings.

The Spaldings came to New Salem, soon to be renamed "Conneaut," in 1809. They had previously lived in Cherry Valley, New York, where Spalding had an unsuccessful run as a store owner.

Shortly after their arrival, Reverend Spalding's health declined, and he retired. To pass the time, he explored the mounds and fortifications along Conneaut Creek. For Spalding and other curious New Salem residents, poking around these relics was a fascinating pastime because of the artifacts they yielded.

At some point, Spalding's interest in the relics jumped the line between fact and conjecture. He began to write a historical romance about the discovery of America by Romans, centuries before Columbus. This document became known as "Manuscript Story—Conneaut Creek."

Spalding's source for this story was a cache of parchment rolls that he found in a cave along Conneaut Creek. Quoting from the opening chapter:

> *Near the west bank of the Coneaught* [sic] *River there are the remains of an ancient fort. As I was walking and forming various conjectures respecting the character, situation & numbers of those people who far exceeded the present Indians in work of art and ingenuity, I happened to tread on a flat stone. This was at a small distance from the fort & it lay on the top of a small mound of Earth exactly horizontal. The face of it had a singular appearance. I discovered a number of characters which appeared to me to be letters, but so much effaced by the ravages of time, that I could not read the inscription.*

Spalding describes how the stone concealed the opening to a cave, in which he discovered an "earthen Box with a cover which shut it perfectly tite." Inside were at least twenty-four rolls of manuscripts on parchment, written using Roman letters and the Latin language.

While the text covered a variety of subjects, the one Spalding singled out for his discourse was "a history of the author's life & that part of America which extends along the great Lakes & the waters of the Mississippy."

Spalding worked on his book for three years, and as each chapter developed, he shared the narrative with his brother, John; former business partner, Henry Lake; and neighbors, all of whom took a great interest in the work.

"The neighbors would often inquire how Mr. Spalding progressed in deciphering the manuscript; and when he had sufficient portion prepared, he would inform them, and they would assemble to hear it read," wrote his widow in 1839. "He was enabled from his acquaintance with the classics and ancient history, to introduce many singular names, which were particularly noticed by the people, and could be easily recognized by them."

"He told me his object was to account for all the fortifications, &c. to be found in this country, and said that in time it would be fully believed by all, except learned men and historians," stated Aaron Wright in a sworn statement made at Conneaut in August 1833.

The Spaldings moved from New Salem to Pittsburgh about the time Solomon Spalding completed his manuscript. He died of tuberculosis in 1816 in Amity, Washington County, Pennsylvania.

Spalding's historical romance novels, hardly masterpieces of literature, would have been forgotten had it not been for the publication of the Book of

Fort Hill, south of Conneaut, rises abruptly above the Conneaut Creek Valley. The natural formation was used as a fortification by a prior culture in this region and is one of several such fortifications discovered by settlers in the Western Reserve. *Author's collection.*

Mormon, which followers of the Church of Jesus Christ, Latter-Day Saints, consider to be "another testament of Jesus Christ."

The Mormon book claims to be a record of peoples in ancient America. Moroni, the last of the Nephite prophets, visited Joseph Smith in 1823 and subsequently allowed Smith to access the buried plates and translate its "reformed Egyptian" characters using a special stone, also provided by Moroni. The Book of Mormon was published in 1830.

Mormonism spread quickly through the Western Reserve, where Joseph Smith built his temple in Kirtland. In 1832, two missionaries, Samuel H. Smith and Orson Hyde, ventured into Conneaut and began sharing from the Book of Mormon. Their readings ignited a controversy and brought forth charges of plagiarism by the old-timers, including John Spalding, Solomon's brother, who had followed his sibling's efforts to "translate" the scrolls he found in the cave. Smith's "revelations" sounded like old news, right down to the names of the characters in the story.

Lake, Spalding's business partner, testified that he was "astonished to find the same passages in it that Spalding had read to me more than twenty years before from his 'Manuscript Found.'"

A former employee, John Miller, and several former neighbors—Aaron Wright, O. Smith, Nahum Howard and Artemus Cunningham—made statements affirming the parallels between the Mormon book and Spalding's original manuscript. At least eight Conneaut residents who knew Spalding when he lived there signed affidavits attesting to Spalding's authorship of a book with passages identical to the Book of Mormon. John Spalding's testimony reads:

> *I have recently read the Book of Mormon, and to my great surprise I find nearly the same historical matter, names &c. as they were in my brother's writings. I well remember that he wrote in the old style, and commenced about every sentence with "and it came to pass," or "now it came to pass," the same as in the Book of Mormon, and according to the best of my recollection and belief, it is the same as my brother Solomon wrote, with the exception of the religious matter.—By what means it has fallen into the hands of Joseph Smith Jr. I am unable to determine.*

"The excitement in New Salem became so great that the inhabitants had a meeting and deputed Dr. Philastus Hurlburt, one of their number, to repair to this place, and to obtain from me the original manuscript of Mr. Spalding, for the purpose of comparing it with the Mormon Bible, to satisfy their own minds, and to prevent their friends from embracing an error so delusive," Matilda Spalding wrote in her 1839 commentary on the matter.

Hurlburt had been an elder in the nascent faith but fell out of favor, setting him on a mission to discredit Joseph Smith's claims. But the manuscript that Matilda Spalding presented to Hurlburt was not the story that the Conneaut residents recalled—or, at least, the manuscript that Hurlburt showed to the Conneaut residents was not the one they remembered. Some believe that Matilda Spalding sent both manuscripts, "Manuscript Found" and "Manuscript Story," to Hurlburt, but he surrendered the controversial document to Smith, who destroyed it.

That seems unlikely, however, for Hurlburt continued his work on an anti-Mormon treatise, *Mormonism Unvailed* (*sic*), which he sold to E.D. Howe of Painesville.

Howe tracked down Matilda Spalding and once again requested the original manuscript, which she sent. Again, the document that Howe reviewed did not resemble the Book of Mormon or resonate with the recollections of the Conneaut residents. The whereabouts of the document that Spalding wrote while in Conneaut, "Manuscript Found," and shared with his family and neighbors was as much a mystery as the mounds that inspired it.

A theory developed based on Matilda Spalding's recollection of her husband's depositing a manuscript with a Mr. Patterson in Pittsburgh, who did not see any value in publishing it. Around 1818, Mr. Patterson went into partnership with a Mr. Lambdin. Patterson recalled that, in 1823, a "wandering preacher" by the name of Sidney Rigdon arrived in Pittsburgh and struck up a friendship with Lambdin.

The manuscript deposited with Patterson was never returned. Further, Mrs. Spalding claimed that a second, complete copy of it came up missing from her trunk while she was living in Ontario County, New York, next door to a man for whom Joe Smith was digging a well.

Ridgon,[24] thus implicated with Oliver Cowdrey as the true authors of the Book of Mormon, called those stories "the most base of lies, without even the shadow of truth." Further, Rigdon maintained that he did not meet Joseph Smith until 1830, when Rigdon was converted in Mentor, Ohio, by the testimony of two missionaries from Palmyra, New York.

According to the faith, Cowdrey is one of the "Three Witnesses" chosen by the Lord to view the gold plates that Joseph Smith found. Cowdrey prepared practically all of the Book of Mormon for the printer and swore that he saw the golden plates from which Joseph Smith translated the book.

The surviving manuscript passed to a Mr. Rice, who published antislavery newspapers. He eventually moved to Honolulu to live with his daughter, a graduate of Oberlin College. President Fairchild of the college visited the alumnus in 1885 and asked for a donation of antislavery material for the college library. Spalding's manuscript was discovered among the papers and donated to Oberlin, where it remains to this day. It has become known as the "Oberlin Manuscript." The document has been studied extensively for its similarities to the Book of Mormon and Spalding/Rigdon authorship. Even sophisticated software has been used to study the story similarities and evidence of the writing styles of Spalding, Rigdon and Cowdrey in the Book of Mormon. Each study seems to contradict the previous; for readers who are interested in further information, there are several websites devoted to the controversy. The only constant in the debate appears to be a lack of consistency from study to study.

For the record, the LDS Church officially dismisses as being without credit what has been termed the "Spalding-Rigdon theory of Book of Mormon authorship." As for the missing "Manuscript Found," it is, like the gold plates that Joseph Smith said he surrendered to Moroni after translating them for the Book of Mormon, hidden history, awaiting rediscovery.

5
DISGUISES

Some people have good reason to hide their identity—spies, for example, and odd ducks. No, that should be "Bucks."

First the spy, Elizabeth Brown Stiles.

She was a daughter of John "Corker" and Clarissa Brown. Corker's nickname was a reference to his occupation, caulking ships. The Brown farm was on the east side of the Ashtabula River, in the area south of present-day Route 20, Ashtabula Township.

Born on August 21, 1816, Elizabeth learned life skills from both parents. From Corker, she learned how to shoot a gun and ride horseback better than most boys; indeed, by the age of five, she had an accurate aim with her gun. Her mother, a "born nurse," taught Elizabeth how to keep her composure in an emergency as well as tend to the sick and dying.

At the age of twenty-one, Elizabeth, full of confidence and skilled as a nurse, teacher and seamstress, headed to Chicago. Her skill set allowed her to support herself in the city, and it was after being there for nine years that she married Jacob Stiles.

One of Elizabeth's sisters, Emeline Dolph, died in 1858, leaving two children, Clara and George, in Kansas City. Jacob and Elizabeth adopted the niece and nephew, as well as another child, Sara. And in 1859, the family moved to Shawneetown, Kansas.

On the Kansas-Missouri border, Shawneetown was in a section frequented by outlaws, such as the Charles Quantrill gang. At issue was whether or not Kansas ought to be a free or slave state. Both Elizabeth and Jacob were patriotic and loyal to the Union. Elizabeth, a teacher, demonstrated her personal values by carrying an American flag at the head of a procession of students, who followed her to the village flagpole. She was threatened by a man along the route—if she repeated this show of patriotism to the Union, the teacher could expect a coat of tar and feathers.

The next morning, Elizabeth and the students repeated their march to the flagpole.

There were no tar and feathers. But that night, in October 1862, as the Stiles family slumbered in their beds, there was a knock at the door. Elizabeth was first to answer. A group of men appearing to be Federal soldiers sought directions, specifically from Jacob. Elizabeth woke up her husband, who was called into the yard for the discussion.

"What's your politics?" asked George Todd of Kansas City, one of Quantill's gang disguised as soldiers.

"Union," Jacob said.

The outlaw shot him on the spot, in front of Elizabeth and the children.

A neighbor by the name of Palmer, approached Jacob's body, placed the muzzle of his weapon to Jacob's mouth and shot him again.

One of the guerrillas seized Elizabeth and put a gun to her head. She was recognized as a nurse who had cared for wounded and sick Union soldiers. The guerrilla was determined to end her life, as well, but Quantrill intervened.

"Let her go, boys. She's too pretty to shoot," Quantrill barked.

Elizabeth and the three children found refuge at Fort Leavenworth. Elizabeth Stiles was well known to the blue army's officers as both a nurse and an informant. Her notoriety reached all the way to the White House, which issued an invitation for her meet with President Lincoln. He had "important work for her to do."

She met the president in August 1863 and received her commission as a military nurse.[25] Her true mission, however, would be to spy on the Confederates.

Elizabeth's disguise was that of a pipe-smoking old Southern woman looking for her wounded son. For the role of her granddaughter, and daughter of the wounded soldier, she chose her eldest daughter, Clara, who was thirteen. The rest of her disguise consisted of a granny cap and powder to turn her hair gray. Tucked into a deep pocket of her full skirt was the letter that President Lincoln wrote to Secretary of War Stanton requesting Stiles's commission.

Behind enemy lines, Elizabeth went to work in taverns and hospitals. While the doctors whom she assisted were busy with their patients,

Right: Elizabeth Stiles in her Southern-grandmother spy outfit. *Ashtabula County Historical Society collection.*

Below: The grave of Elizabeth Stiles is in the pauper's section of Middle Ridge Cemetery in Madison. Stiles was a native of Ashtabula and served as a spy in the American Civil War. *Author's collection.*

Elizabeth poked about their medicine bags, where sensitive information was often hidden in a secret pocket or envelope. In taverns, Elizabeth discovered that buying a couple rounds of whiskey for loose-lipped soldiers often paid dividends of war stories and strategies.

Her work took her into the worst of situations. On one occasion, the only way to spy on a nighttime meeting of officers was to listen through a crack between the boards of a dilapidated house where the gathering was held. To reach the spot of inquiry, Elizabeth had to crouch in a hog pen, where she spent the night with the pen's occupants. Mission accomplished.

Although her disguise was convincing, it was not foolproof. Elizabeth was arrested in Jefferson City, Missouri, on suspicion of being a Union spy. She was brought before General Price, who questioned her at length. Elizabeth had acquired both a Southern accent and vast knowledge of the South's geography and military strongholds; she drew on information to convince the general that she was a Confederate spy. At the end of the interrogation, Price was so convinced of her identity he stood up and apologized for delaying her work.

Price ordered a meal for her, a fresh horse and better firearms before sending her back into the field.

Her daughter told the story of falling asleep on her horse as she and Elizabeth traveled by night on the Kansas-Missouri border. A sentry grasped the head of Elizabeth's horse as they passed a picket line and attempted to arrest Elizabeth. The sound of a gunshot woke up Clara, who noticed the picket line was short one sentry.

These stories were shared by Elizabeth and Clara in the years following the war. Elizabeth lived with her son, George, in Venango, Pennsylvania, until 1895, when she entered the Women's Relief Corps Home in Madison.

She died on July 18, 1898, and, despite her war hero status, was buried in the home's very modest cemetery nearby. Her grave is marked with a simple stone, her history, like her wartime identity, hidden.

SOUL MATES

On the east side of Conneaut, in what was probably the first brick house in the village once known as "New Hope," lived one of the most eccentric characters this city has ever known. And that's saying something, considering this town was home to Axis Sally!

Samuel Buck departed this life on May 21, 1871, at an "advanced age," most likely in his eighties. The news of his death was published in the *Cincinnati Daily Gazette* and *Elkhart Weekly Review*, the latter headlining the story as "The Funny Man of Conneaut."

Samuel certainly earned the title, as did his wife, Mrs. Buck, who died the same day he did. Indeed, she passed away the same minute, fulfilling the prophecy that Buck often told to visitors: "When she dies, I die; When I die, she dies."

Frank J. Cheney, who was a young schoolteacher in the village during Buck's senior years, wrote about the couple's strange connection in *A Life of Unity, and Other Stories*, published in 1901. Cheney shares his visits with Mr. and Mrs. Buck, who were never in the same room at the same time.

Much of the story is devoted to Mr. Buck's narrow views on marriage and divorce.

"No pure-minded Christian people who fear God, have nothing but good in their hearts and marry for love, ever think of divorce," Buck told Cheney. "It is a violation of the most sacred law."

Later in the conversation, Buck said, "So you will see we have a union founded in heaven on the divine laws, and we are virtually living a life of unity, without any restrictions or hindrance—a life which allows each to execute the work laid out for us. I have Mrs. Buck's full co-operation in everything I undertake, and therefore no failure."

And Samuel Buck undertook a lot of ventures. The lawns of his property were immaculately and artistically maintained; his garden grew rare flowers, foliage and fruit. He manufactured wood type used in printing presses and had a "curiosity shop," wherein he worked with surveying instruments, sun dials and other paraphernalia of the mathematician, artist and engineer. According to Cheney, Buck worked for the government and produced "the most perfect hand drawings I had ever seen."

Cheney visited Samuel Buck in the morning. Samuel invited him back that evening to visit with Mrs. Buck, a woman about sixty years old. "She had large blue eyes and a good face, voice pleasing to hear, except at times perhaps a little heavy or masculine," he wrote.

Mrs. Buck described her role as the housekeeper who fulfilled her duty to ensure a "quiet, pleasant home, free from disturbances and trouble," for her husband.

"Mr. Buck tells me everything he does or thinks," she told Cheney. Any purchase that either spouse contemplated was reviewed by the other.

Reflecting on his visits, Cheney concluded that "I never saw such a man before in my life, and such a character." "He gives the divorce laws no quarter. I wonder if he has ever been jilted or had any experience that set him so against them. He says that his marriage is registered in heaven—no human law married him. Is it possible that they are not married? That would be awful."

Cheney noted that Samuel was about the same height as his wife and had the same color eyes. He thought that they were brother and sister, which made Buck's talk about marriage even more disturbing. The next day, Buck told Cheney that his spouse was born the same day he was, to the minute. Later that evening, he visited with Mr. and Mrs. Buck, but not at the same time or in the same room. He parted with Mrs. Buck, who was admiring her new outfit in the mirror. She assured him that Mr. Buck, if he were feeling better, would be working in the garden the next day.

"I called the next day and saw Mr. Buck sitting at the window. He said he had been ill all night; and there was nothing I could do for him. I knew he was in good hands, as Mrs. Buck would attend to him," Cheney wrote.

"I called the next day. There was a crape on the door. A neighbor was there and told me that Mr. Buck had died about two o'clock that morning. I inquired about Mrs. Buck, and he said she died at the same time.

"Mr. and Mrs. Buck had in truth lived a life of unity. They were the one and same person," Cheney concluded.

His death notice in the *Conneaut Reporter* of May 25, 1871, simply stated that "Mr B. was a bachelor and had lived by himself for many years and was a man of great eccentricity especially in the point of dress, preferring the habiliments of a woman to those of his sex, and quite often Miss as Mr. Buck could be found at home attired in the fineries of the season."

The *Cincinnati Daily Gazette*'s story, which was picked up from the *Erie Republican*, explained Buck's strange story in these terms:

> *Years ago he formed an attachment for a lady, made an avowal, and was rejected. The young woman (for he was young at that time) was not prepared for such a rendering of affairs, and without even a remonstrance at his charmer's decision gave up the society of the fair sex once and forever, purchased a sequestered spot, remote from the haunts of man or the prying eyes of woman, reared a cot, staked out his earthly domain and settled down into a state of ultra "single blessedness."*
>
> *...After rearing his house and furnishing it with the comforts for which the heart of man longeth, he proceeded to create from his own rib and person a woman, by allowing his hair to grow long, and the purchase of a complete wardrobe of female apparel, and from that time forward, when*

> *"at home," he designated himself as Miss Buck, and never appeared in another character, unless someone called, as was sometimes the case, and asked for Mr. Buck.*

Having no children, Buck's curious belongings, and fine clothes, went to a nephew who lived in Michigan. The Bucks' brick house, which was later covered with stucco and thus made quite unattractive, no longer stands in East Conneaut.

6

Tinker Hollow

Conneaut Creek, a state Wild and Scenic River, hides its history well.

Few people who drop a line in this excellent steelhead creek know that Captain Sam Ward launched his shipbuilding career on this stream in 1818 with the launching of the *Salem Packet.* Ward was an enterprising Great Lakes captain and the taproot for the "Ward Empire" of shipbuilding that was perpetuated by his nephew, Eber Ward. He became the wealthiest man in Michigan and was declared the "King of the Lakes." He also was the father of Princese de Caraman-Chimay, better known as Clara Ward to the folks back in Conneaut, where the spunky teenager spent her summers.

After her father's death, Clara devoted the rest of her life to exhausting his fortune. Her conduct, too raunchy for even New York City, led her to France, where she found her trophy husband, Prince Joseph de Caraman-Chimay. He gave her a title; she gave him the cash to get out of debt and rebuild his crumbling château in Belgium.

Clara bore two children for the prince, grew bored of the château life and went looking for love in Paris. She jumped ship and ran away with a gypsy violinist. A divorce ensued, and Clara and her lover spent the next few years spending money and creating a sensation wherever they appeared. Her beauty was deemed so "disturbing" by Kaiser Wilhelm II that he banned the publication or display of her photograph in the German Empire.

Back in Conneaut, where her uncle started building his fortune, the Tinker family was creating their fortune in a dark hollow of Conneaut Creek. Bog iron, water and hardwoods, from which charcoal could be made, drew

The Tinker Foundry was showing its age when this photograph was made around 1929, the year the business ceased operations. *Kingsville Public Library collection.*

the enterprising Tinker brothers, William and Sylvester, to the Conneaut Creek hollow, where they built a foundry that is shrouded in mystery.

The brothers' first iron cupola furnace was built around 1835 on the ridge above the river valley. Furnaces of this design were built wherever bog iron deposits were sufficient to support an iron-making industry. Conneaut had this ore and associated industry along Furnace Road, as did Harpersfield Township, where the Clyde Iron Furnace stood. And farther west, along the North Ridge in Madison Township, the Arcole Iron Works quickly grew to become the largest manufacturing facility in Ohio in the early 1830s.[26]

The Arcole Works employed two thousand men in 1831, two hundred of whom had the task of producing the charcoal for the furnaces. A dock was constructed north of the ironworks at Lake Erie for shipping the output to Buffalo. The ironworks, founded in 1825, continued until 1852, when it was abandoned for want of ore.

Bog iron has a relatively low concentration of iron in its substance, usually no more than 25 percent. It is formed in bogs through a chemical reaction that leaches out the iron dissolved in ground water.

This undated photograph shows members of the Tinker family, with the machine shop on the left and the foundry on the right in the background. *Author's collection.*

The crude but effective cupola furnace was made of stone or brick, stood thirty-two feet or taller and was usually square at the base. It was situated on the flats below a hillside, which facilitated dumping the raw materials into the furnace from the top.

Layers of ore, charcoal and limestone, the fluxing agent, were added and a charge set to ignite the charcoal. It would take roughly three tons of ore, one and a half tons of limestone and 265 bushels of charcoal to yield one ton of iron. The furnace operated around the clock; periodically, the molten ore and slag were pulled from the bottom. The iron flowed into troughs to form sow bars (pig iron) or into molds to make cast iron products.

The Tinker furnaces never attained the output of those at Arcole; the Tinkers focused on producing iron for farm implements and tools. And whereas Arcole employed two thousand men, employment at the Tinker Foundry amounted to only several dozen workers at its peak. But each Tinker employee knew how to perform every job. That included casting every part, right down to the nuts and bolts that held together the machinery and other cast-iron items the factory made.[27] And workers were well compensated for their efforts, making two to three dollars per day in gold, which was the Tinker brothers' preferred method of payment for their products, as well.

The Tinker operation, out of necessity, also included shops, in which the patterns for their metal products were fashioned from wood. They harnessed

The foundry patterns from Tinker's Hollow are owned by the Ashtabula County Historical Society. The wooden pattern was pressed into damp sand to make the impression that received the molten metal. *Author's collection.*

the power of Conneaut Creek with a dam, a section of which is still visible, and used that power to turn the lathes and other shop equipment. By the 1850s, the bog iron supply petered out; however, iron became available through the Port of Conneaut, and the Tinkers hauled it to the hollow on a horse-drawn cart.

The 1850s saw the development of numerous mowing machines by inventors in Ohio and elsewhere. Some of the early successes in the Buckeye State included the Ketchum, which appeared in Champaign County in 1848, and the Ohio, manufactured by Ball, Aultman & Co. of Canton. The most innovative and successful mowers had a hinged cutter bar and two drive wheels.

The Tinker brothers also designed and built a mowing machine. Eschewing the trend toward two drive wheels, the Tinker design used a single drive wheel, which drove a cutter bar. The whole thing sat on a triangular frame.

None of these horse-drawn machines has survived,[28] so we must rely on descriptions provided by the historian Walter Jack, who evidently saw one at work prior to writing his article in 1929.

> *The driver was seated behind the* [forty-inch] *wheel. A "S" shaped track was cast just inside the rim of the large drive wheel and a ball at the end of the lever followed this track as the wheel turned. The in and out movement in the "S" imparted the horizontal motion to the section bar. The bar and cam motion was noisy, but not as noisy as many* [other machines] *of the time. It pulled easier than the early machines, but not as easily as the Champion, Wood or Buckeye that came into general use after the Civil War. The motion of the section bar was slower, yet the swath was much wider than the machine of those early years. The Tinker mower cut a four-and-one-half foot swatch, while other machines cut four feet.*

William Tinker gambled his fifteen-acre farm and modest home on the success of this machine. His neighbors gossiped that the mower would be the inventor's ruin. They changed their song when orders for the machines, which cost between $125 and $150 each, started arriving. The Tinker brothers went from fools to geniuses in the eyes of their neighbors. Within a year, they had paid off their debts and had begun making improvements to the foundry and shops.

William was the inventor and Sylvester the salesman of this team. He would load a half dozen mowers on a long wagon, hitch his team and head to the farms of Andover, Kinsman or Jefferson. Finding a hayfield where a dozen men were laboring with scythes, Sylvester would unload a machine and hook up the team. Like Santa, he spoke not a word but went right to his work.

He drove the team and mower around the field three times, unhooked the horses and started to load the machine back on the wagon. By that time, a crowd would have gathered, and those sweet words were in the air, "How much?" It's said Tinker seldom left a demonstration without making at least one sale. Sometimes, he'd barter for goods or accept a promissory note.

While effective, Sylvester's marketing approach made for a regional phenomenon and nothing more. Sales figures from the secretive family are nonexistent, but newspaper accounts have suggested that in the foundry's "hay days," it sold between thirty and five hundred annually. The lower number is probably more accurate, as the foundry employed, at most, sixty men and every part had to be cast individually in casting sand, most likely obtained from the sand barrens in Kingsville Township. The higher number is probably a total for the number of units produced.

The brothers invested their profits in a "showcase" home in the valley. Stone was hauled from the creek and brick made from the clay deposits

The Tinker home was well built and quite spacious for its time. When the family left the hollow in 1929, squatters moved in and thieves helped themselves to the windows, doors and other items. *Kingsville Public Library collection.*

in the valley. One Tinker in-law recalled the house having twelve rooms and a cellar.

William also invented a small, stationary threshing machine, the Tinker Pepper Mill, powered by a horse-driven apparatus, also a Tinker invention. Drag saws, operated by a "single, well-trained docile horse," were in the Tinker product line, and the factory turned out hundreds of wood-and-metal apple slicers. These were purchased by women during the Civil War, facilitating a dried apples cottage industry for many women who were left without a means of support while their husbands and sons were fighting in the war.

By 1870, the Tinker Mowing Machine was eclipsed by much better designs. The foundry continued to produce replacement parts and manufactured plow points, the business end of the plow that makes contact with the soil and rocks. For a point to do its job and last, it had to be sharp; typical cast-iron points did neither thing very well, but there was something about the Tinker iron that made their points last and stay sharp longer.

One newspaper article claimed that a Tinker plow point could do 250 acres whereas the competitor's would be worn out after just 70. The Tinker's point was less expensive and had a distinctive ring that compared to that of a "fine-toned bell."

This unusual hardness of Tinker iron led to rumors of a secret ingredient and/or a mysterious step in the process that imparted these qualities.[29] Combined with the secluded, hollow setting of their foundry and stories of suicide and murders therein, the name "Tinker" became associated with legends and ghost stories.

One of those legends is easily dispelled. For years, it was said that the livid metal markers erected over the graves of Tinker family members were made from a Tinker iron that does not rust. True, there is no rust on those markers after more than one hundred years of exposure to the elements, but they are made of zinc, not iron, as is easily demonstrated with a magnet. Further, the markers are hardly unique to the Tinkers and most old cemeteries have at least one or two of them. If anything, the markers are a testimony to the brothers' propensity for a bargain; sold by Monumental Bronze, the markers were relatively inexpensive yet allowed for a high degree of detail in the castings. The markers were popular for about ten years, peaking in the late 1880s, and then quickly fell out of favor. In the public's eye, "cheap" was associated with inferior, something you don't want for a loved one's memorial; some cemeteries even went so far as to ban the markers. The Tinker family, however, embraced their value.

There remains, however, the legend of the hard steel. A man who worked for the Tinker Foundry claimed that the Tinkers used a secret ingredient that was kept in a brown bag. When no one was watching, the owner would removed a pinch of the substance from the bag in his back pocket and add it to the mix.

This claim was dismissed by Fred Tinker in an interview the author conducted in 1998. Fred was the son of William Tinker Jr., the last family member to operate the foundry. William took the secret, if there was one, to the grave with him, although he revealed in a 1929 newspaper article that he showed a curious visitor the family secret.

> *"One man came in here from the X—— Plow Company, one of the largest. He was dressed up, diamonds on his fingers. I knew he didn't belong around here," William Jr. told the reporter. "He asked if he could come in. I told him 'sure'...He watched for a long time. Finally he said, 'I'd like to know how you do that.'*

"I said, 'We'll I'll tell you. I pour from this side of the ladle, then from the other side. The iron that comes out of this side is just ordinary, but the other side is hard as steel.'

"He said, 'Ah, what causes that?' So I told him, 'Well, you see, that side of the ladle is cold.'"

The Tinker Foundry went out of business in 1929. At that point, William Jr. was the only family member still involved. William Jr. was the son of Julius and Susan (Close) Tinker, and Julius was the son of Sylvester Jr., who purchased William Sr.'s share of the business around 1870.

Nothing of Tinker Hollow remains aboveground, although in the winter, one might make out the foundation of the old homestead. The old iron bridge that crossed the river has been abandoned and closed by the county, and the area, a pristine section of Conneaut Creek, is privately held. A favorite spot for lusty, backseat encounters, the ghost legends, not to mention

Brickwork at the Tinker foundry was still standing when this image was made in the middle of the twentieth century. *Kingsville Public Library collection.*

surveillance efforts by the property owner, have a way of tossing cold water on hot moments.

One source of these ghost stories has nothing to do with the Tinkers. It is said you can hear a one-legged man walking across the deck of the old iron bridge late at night. There was a handicapped man who lived in the hollow, a vagrant who took up residence in the Tinker home after the family abandoned the hollow. The man had been struck by lightning at some time in his life, causing the limp.

Another story has Silas Tinker, the father of Sylvester Sr., haunting the hollow. If you run across Silas in the dark, he will lead you to his cache of gold. Just look for the glowing, green eyes, but be careful not to confuse them with the property owner's security cameras!

7

Unmarked Graves

Not all graves are marked, even those in the cemeteries.

In fact, the grave of a famous Ashtabula County citizen is neither marked nor in a cemetery. It is very close to one, however.

The grave is that of Buster, a farm dog whose story of faithfulness to his master was told in more than fifty newspapers and commands several pages in a book about amazing dogs. Born in 1921 on the farm/orchard of Perry and Lena VanCourt near Conneaut, Buster was one of at least five pups examined by James and Mary VanCourt before they made their selection. The VanCourts, originally from Richey County, West Virginia, had migrated to the flat farmland of Richmond Township some six years earlier. They farmed the land just west of the township cemetery and lived in a big white house across the pasture that separated them from the realm of the dead.

A skilled horse handler, James VanCourt had no problem training Buster to perform his herding, driving and watchdog chores about the farm. "He grew into an ideal farm dog with [a] massive chest and heavy coat and became the best cow driver in the township," noted a newspaper article. The tan-and-white collie proved to be not only a bright credit to his species but also a faithful one.

"Dad would say, 'Buster, go get the bull,' and he'd bring up the bull. Or he'd say, 'Buster, go get the horses,' and he'd bring up the horses," said the VanCourts' grandson, Jim VanCourt, in a 2003 interview for the *Ashtabula Star Beacon*.

Buster's mother looks on as VanCourt family members admire the puppies. It is likely one of those pups was the famed Buster. *Penny Redmond collection.*

Jim grew up about a half mile from his grandparents' farm and, along with his father, Richard, worked on the property with Buster at his side.

"Every morning, Dad would say, 'Come on son, we got to go milk cows.' I used to walk behind him to help break the cold wind," Jim VanCourt said.

As a youngster, Jim used Buster's intelligence to his own advantage. If Jim had to round up the cows for the evening milking, he would get a milk bucket from the barn and rattle it near Buster, and the dog would take over from there.

"He'd hear that pail rattling and away he'd go," Jim VanCourt said.

Buster was protective of his family, and he would stand between Mary VanCourt and any stranger who approached the farm. He also kept the ornery roosters at bay.

"My grandmother had this old rooster that would get me cornered. She'd say, 'Buster, get him!' Boy, the feathers would fly then. He was quite a dog," VanCourt recalled.

As amazing as Buster was during his first seven years of service to the VanCourts, his greatest mettle came with the death of his master in 1928. James VanCourt died of a lingering illness, and throughout that time, Buster lay by his master's side. And then came the passing and the funeral procession to the nearby cemetery.

James and Mary VanCourt pose in this undated photograph. *Penny Redmond collection.*

Buster followed this procession as he had followed his master to the barn on so many frigid mornings. And after the dirt was mounded on the grave and the mourners departed for the funeral dinner, Buster curled up on the grave and began eight years of mourning.

Day after day, Buster remained on the mound, despite the daily visit and coaxing of Mary VanCourt. He ate and drank little of the sustenance she brought him.

Word of the collie's dedication spread beyond the farming hamlet, and Buster's story began appearing in local and regional newspapers. Curious folks visited the grave to see this grieving canine, pat his head and perhaps offer a treat. But as with all losses and curiosities that occur beyond our immediate circle of connects, Buster was soon forgotten. Yet when the sight of a farm dog starving himself on the grave of his master was no longer a novelty and the crowds no longer visited, Buster stayed.

On some unrecorded resurrection morning, Buster woke up very lonely and hungry. He rose from the mound and trotted down the hill to the farmhouse. His arrival was greeted with the family's joy, a hearty breakfast and a long drink at the watering tub.

His body thus nourished, Buster returned to his tasks of herding and watchdogging. But when his duties were done at the end of day, Buster cast his brown eyes toward the knoll, trotted across the pasture, crawled under the wire fence between field and cemetery and curled up on his master's grave, where he slept throughout the night.

The next morning, Buster was back at the farmhouse, ready to begin his duties.

This became Buster's life: Work the farm when duty called, climb the hill to the cemetery when grief overwhelmed. His trips, always taken along the same direct route from farmhouse to grave, "made afresh each season a well-worn path across fields of summer grain and winter snow," according to a newspaper article published in 1932.

The years of sleeping in wintry torment, of barking his commands at the cows and living with a heavy heart finally took their toll on Buster. Likewise, Mary VanCourt suffered poor health that often confined her to the same room where her husband's life had slipped away.

Buster transferred his vigil to his master's widow, choosing a spot outside the kitchen door, where he could monitor her well-being while keeping an eye on the grave across the pasture. His trips to the grave became less frequent as arthritis afflicted his joints and time clouded his once-bright eyes.

The graves of VanCourt family members face the farm and pasture where Buster once roamed. Legend has it that Buster was buried in his master's toolbox on the pasture side of the fence. *Author's collection.*

On March 31, 1936, Buster attempted one more trip to the grave of his master, but his tired body could not make the pilgrimage. Family members found him collapsed in the meadow. They carried him to the back porch of the farmhouse, where he lay whimpering and crying throughout the night, "his shaggy head between feeble forepaws," as one newspaper writer put it.

At 4:00 a.m. on April 1, Mary VanCourt awoke and, as had become her habit, listened for Buster's whimper. All was quiet, except the sound of the wind encountering the cemetery knoll.

Jim VanCourt's father and an uncle, Clyde, buried Buster later that morning, at the eastern edge of the farm. Mary VanCourt requested that this beloved, faithful dog be buried near her husband's grave, at the opening in the fence where he had entered the cemetery every evening.

His coffin was a treasured wooden toolbox that had belonged to his master. But no stone marks his grave, and life has reclaimed the paths that his treasured paws wore in this landscape during the commission of his duties.

Mary VanCourt died in 1945. The farm passed to Clyde VanCourt and then to his son, Syd, who died in 2000. Jim VanCourt, probably the last family member who had a personal recollection of Buster, died in January 2011.

Buster's stories of faithfulness and passing were printed in dozens of newspapers, and his biography was included in *A Book of Famous Dogs* by Albert Payson Terhune.

A VICTIM OF WINTER

Animals are not the only creatures to be interred in unmarked spots. For example, the first child of European descent to die in the Western Reserve was buried "in the woods" near the Conneaut Creek. It's likely the grave was destroyed during construction of harbor and dock facilities.

It was the winter of 1796–97. All but a few members of the first survey party of the Western Reserve Land Company had completed their work and returned to Connecticut. At Cleveland, what there was of it, Job and Tabitha Stiles hunkered down to ride out the winter with help from their Native American neighbors, who provided game. At Salem (Conneaut), where the survey party made its initial landing in the Reserve on July 4 of that year, James Kingsbury; his wife, Eunice; their nephew; and their three children planned to spend the winter in the survey party's former supply store near Conneaut Creek.

In the fall of 1796, after making the decision to winter over in New Connecticut, James Kingsbury left his family in the homestead while he returned to New Hampshire. Kingsbury expected a trip of six weeks, which, in theory, would have put him back in the Reserve before the worst of the winter weather descended, or so he thought.

He became ill with the fever, blamed on the "malarial swamps" of Conneaut, and was forced to spend several weeks recuperating rather than traveling. Once he had recovered sufficiently to travel again, he rode for three weeks through snow up to five feet deep. From Buffalo, New York, to Erie, Pennsylvania, an Indian guide helped him find his way back to the crude shelter near the lakeshore.

At Presque Isle, Pennsylvania, Kingsbury purchased twenty pounds of flour. As his horse crossed the frozen Elk Creek, the animal became disabled, and Kingsbury had to abandon it. Kingsbury pressed on toward the mouth of Conneaut Creek.

He arrived on Christmas Eve to find his emaciated wife on a cot, ill with fever. Next to her were the remains of the infant. The family's cow had died from browsing on oak trees. Without food to eat, Eunice Kingbury could not nurse the infant, and he soon died of starvation.

James Kingsbury found a wooden box left behind by the surveyors and transformed it into a coffin for his infant son. Then he walked into the forest and buried the box.

There was no time for mourning. His wife and the children desperately needed nutrition; Kingsbury dragged a sled to the closest settlement—some accounts say Cleveland, others, Erie, Pennsylvania—where he purchased a bushel of wheat. Back in New Salem, Kingsbury noticed a pigeon in the tree as he sat in the woods one chilly day. He shot the bird and made some broth from its carcass. He served it to his wife, who had been delirious and near death for a fortnight.

"James, where did you get this?" she asked.

Eunice recovered, and when spring arrived, Kingsbury moved what was left of his family to the tiny settlement of Cleveland. Within four years, he was appointed a judge there, and had a long, successful career.

LITTLE JOHN

At the point where Indian Creek and Lake Erie become one, there once lived a Chippewa Indian named Little John.

Little John's tribe was based in Sault St. Marie, but every fall, it returned to the Lake Erie shore to hunt, fish and trap on what were common grounds. The early settlers of Harpersfield came to know and become friends with Little John, who had a wife and several children. Their winter wigwam was on the lakeshore, just east of the present-day village of Geneva-on-the-Lake. As anyone who has spent a winter along Lake Erie might have guessed, Little John and his family were a very hardy lot.

Platt R. Spencer, in the *Record of the Historical and Philosophical Society of Ashtabula County, Ohio*, relates that in 1806 a number of Indians appeared at the home of Major Moses in Harpersfield. The Indians were painted black and obviously suffering deep sorrow. Through gestures, they explained that a fatal accident had occurred and that they wanted the settlers to follow them to a place about eight miles away.

Upon their arrival at the lakeshore, the settlers discovered that Little John had been killed while cutting down a tree in which game was lodged.

Indian Creek in Geneva Township got its name from "Little John," a Chippewa Indian who lived by the creek and was buried there. *Author's collection.*

Sharing in the grief of the family and tribe, the settlers assisted with the burial, which was conducted according to Chippewa tradition.

Little John was buried in a sitting position in a sand bank on the west side of Indian Creek. He was wrapped in his blanket, and his favored possessions were buried with him: a knife, a kettle, flint tender and steel, a hatchet and a rifle. An enclosure of poles was placed around the grave, and a red post was put in the center. The small community grieved for its loss.

Greed eventually overcame grief, however, and grave robbers cheated Little John out of his treasures.

The rifle and kettle were the first to be stolen. Next, an anatomy student swiped his bones. Eventually, the flint and steel were taken. Even the waves of Lake Erie reclaimed the sand bank that had been his grave.

Spencer writes that Little John's bones did find a final resting place in Ashtabula County, however. The anatomy student left the bones at a house in the settlement with the intention of returning for them. He never showed up, and the superstitious wife of the household had them buried on the farm. History does not record that location, but there remains a legend of Little John haunting the creek and forest.

No trace of Little John remains today, except the creek whose name pays homage to his kind and a poem, penned by Spencer and found among his papers by his son, Lyman P.

The Chippewa Chief—Little John

His wild heart throbbed with manly pride;
Free as the winds that sweep the wave,
He ranged the woods by Erie's side,
Or mused above his father's grave.

Freedom he loved—wild, generous, brave,
His soul was wrapt in sylvan scenes,
The chase, the song, the surging wave,
The forest depths and whispering stream.

Where blends you stream with Erie's sea,
The chieftain moored his light canoe,
There through the arms of sheltering tree,
Curled up his wigwam current blue.

There too his humble grave is piled,
Where the strong oak in days of yore,
Firm rooted in the moveless soil,
Bend sombre o'er the sandy shore.

But chieftain, wigwam, tree and grave,
Are gone like some forgotten dream,
And only on the tiny wave,
His memory lives in yonder stream.

UNMARKED-GRAVE ROBBER

While grave robbing is unseemly, body snatching in the nineteenth century was fairly common, as medical schools needed a constant supply of corpses for dissection. Returning to Dr. L.E. Brayman, whom we met during our journey along Stanhope-Kelloggsville Road, it has been said that he had a skeleton in his closet, literally.

The late historian Walter Jack relates the story of one George Anderson, born on July 11, 1857, who was willing to do just about anything to become a doctor.

The Anderson family—Sanford, Mary and their children, George, Kate and Frank—lived on a one-hundred-acre farm in the northern section of Pierpont Township on Anderson Road, which terminated at Blodgett's Turnpike. When George was seven, his father attended an evening Union recruitment rally in Steamburg. When the family woke up the next morning, Sanford announced that he had enlisted and marched off to fight in the Civil War that same day.

The burden of running the farm fell on the children and their mother. It is very likely that George knew little of childhood's joys, for his father returned from the war a broken and incapacitated man. Despite the responsibilities placed on his young shoulders, George attended school whenever he could. The daily burden of working on the farm drove him to greater ambitions: George Anderson, MD.

In Anderson's quest to become a physician, it became necessary to study human anatomy firsthand, and that required a cadaver. Jack, in his story, attributes this tale to Dr. Anderson, who was Jack's contemporary and "country neighbor."

Late one fall, a "no-account pauper" who lived in the northwest corner of Richmond Township died and was buried in a graveyard on the east side of Middle Road north of Leon. The pauper was the subject of some town gossip and legends. Some said he refused to take off his belt because it was filled with gold dust that he'd gathered in California. The belt went to the grave with him, of course. And then there were rumors of valuable papers stuffed inside his clothes, which also went in the grave. Even if there were no gold in them thar clothes, there was good reason for a grave robber to be interested in the pauper. Medical schools were paying five dollars for each cadaver, no questions asked.

Anderson saw this as an opportunity to further his education and appealed to Dr. Brayman of Pierpont for assistance; if any person in the community would understand both the necessity of a cadaver and the student's purely academic motives, it was Dr. Brayman. And it turned out that Brayman was sympathetic. Thus, it was agreed that if Anderson could get the body from the cemetery to Pierpont, Brayman would provide a room above his drugstore wherein the studies could be conducted.

It was late November, and the ground in the cemetery was already frozen down several inches when Anderson, cloaked in darkness, arrived with his shovel. He chipped away at the grave but made only a modest dent in the ground. Certain that no one would notice the intrusion—the pauper's grave was in a remote section of the burial ground—Anderson covered the hole with some brush and returned home.

Alas, there was a burial the next day, and the disturbed earth was discovered by the mourners. They concluded that a grave robber was at work, "a crime abhorrent beyond all words," wrote Jack. Word of the disturbance spread through the little community until it reached the drugstore and fell on Dr. Brayman's ears.

"All that talk is damned nonsense, dogs have been digging there," Brayman said.

"Oh yeah," retorted a townsman. "Then how do explain the fact there was brush piled up on that there grave?"

"That's nothing. Dogs can do anything after dark, and I've heard of them gnawing down big trees, trimming them and gnawing them into log lengths better than beavers. They piled the brush, too."

Unconvinced dogs were to blame and suspecting either Brayman or Anderson of being the culprit, several townspeople posted a nighttime watch over the pauper's grave. Eventually, they got tired of waiting, not to mention being very cold, and gave up their watch for the comfort of hearth and bed.

Dr. Brayman's drugstore in Pierpont Township accommodated young George Anderson's interest in human anatomy. *Walter Jack/Ashtabula County Historical Society collection.*

A thaw came around mid-December, and Anderson set out to revisit the grave. He borrowed a horse and two-wheel road cart from the farm and set off toward the cemetery. Once there, he lit his lantern and began searching for the pile of brush. The clay soil was waterlogged and had to be pulled out in large chunks, but he eventually succeeded in reaching the simple, body-fitting coffin.

Anderson, standing in mud and water, heaved the coffin to the surface; all those farm chores that had built up his muscles were finally paying off. Water and mud poured off the box and onto him. Wet to the skin, Anderson arrived at Brayman's place just as the doctor was returning from an all-night vigil at a patient's bedside.

"You damned fool. You'll make a doctor yet," Brayman roared when he saw Anderson. "Let's get the body upstairs before someone comes sneaking around."

The men carried the coffin upstairs. Both men were covered in mud, and Brayman instructed Anderson to get out of his wet clothes, down a bracer and get some sleep. Anderson bedded down on a cot and covered up with horse blankets. One has to wonder what manner of dreams tormented him that night.

It was three miles from Brayman's place to Anderson's farm, but every night that winter, after completing his farm work, Anderson made the trip to Brayman's drugstore, where he and the doctor dissected and studied the corpse.

Dr. George Anderson discovered the benefits of "hot springs" while vacationing and eventually tapped into Andover Village's water, which has a high mineral content, to create his own bathhouse. *Large's History of Ashtabula County.*

Brayman opened his library to the intrepid student and answered Anderson's questions about what he read and saw.

Anderson graduated from the Western Reserve University's medical school in 1884. He returned to Ashtabula County and set up a practice in Williamsfield, where, for five years, he underwent the hardships of being a country doctor. The years of hard work and even grave robbing paid off; Anderson became a leading physician in the county.

In 1883, Dr. Anderson and his wife made a trip to Hot Springs, Arkansas, where they were introduced to the concept of the mineral spring as a healing modality. The springs in Andover, in southeastern Ashtabula County, were known for their mineral content, and Dr. Anderson began mulling over the possibility of starting a bathhouse in that community.

In 1904, Anderson finally opened his sanitarium, Dr. George S. Anderson's Original Hot Springs Bath. It stood just north of the square, on the east side of present-day Route 7. A simplified Italian Provincial house, the sanitarium catered to guests who arrived by train from the Pittsburgh and Youngstown areas. The house was within walking distance of the passenger depot, and to ensure that new arrivals did not miss the place, a huge sign, "HOT SPRINGS BATH HOUSE," occupied the roof ridge and faced the depot.

Originally, the mineral water for this spa came from Sperry's well, which was about three miles from the house and a mile north of where the causeway would be built. As the popularity of the bathhouse grew, demand for the water exceeded Anderson's resources for hauling it. He had his own mineral wells dug on his property, and chemical analysis determined they possessed the same minerals as Sperry's well. Indeed, decades later, water for the village still comes from wells, and the heavy mineral content is a bane to the water plant operators who must deal with the issues those minerals present in treatment and distribution.

Dr. George Anderson's Hot Springs Bath House drew tourists to Andover Village years prior to the construction of the Pymatuning Reservoir. The village's water was infused with minerals that were alleged to impart health and restoration to those who bathed in them. *Author's collection.*

The mineral water was most likely a distant second to Dr. Anderson's "gift" of manipulation (his son, Darl C., became a chiropractor). A typical treatment regimen was two to three weeks in length and involved daily hot baths and massages. The bathtubs were oversized and had feet on them; marble dividers between the tubs provided privacy. The sanitarium had separate sections for men and women; patients embarrassed by bathing au naturel could don a white modesty apron.

Patients paid $2.50 for a bath and massage by Dr. Anderson or one of his trained "rubbers" hired from the local population. At the very least, the guest went away feeling relaxed and, in some cases, healed. Dr. Anderson's poster child for the bathhouse was a person who arrived on crutches and, after a week, was able to throw them away.

"The waters of Dr. G.S. Anderson's Hot Springs Bath House are magnetic, radio active and contain traces of iodine, making them one of the best tonic and alternative waters in the world," declared a brochure promoting the bathhouse.

Anderson's bathhouse proved much more lucrative than delivering babies and patching the mangled limbs of farm workers. He and his staff gave upward of eighty baths a day during the busy season. A $200-a-day take from a small-town business was good money in those days, even one owned by a doctor!

Dr. Norman Osborne went into partnership with Anderson and took over the bathhouse after Anderson's death on January 12, 1924. Dr. George Getz was the last owner of the business, which lasted into the early 1950s. A second bathhouse, owned by Dr. L.M. Uilinger, operated in the Andover Hotel.

In their heyday, these sanitariums were a significant economic engine for the little town. Many of the patients took their meals at the Arlington Hotel, and patients shopped in stores on the village square. The clientele was, in general, well off financially; for many patients, a three-week trip to a mineral springs resort was a vacation in the guise of medical treatment.

Anderson's bathhouse had no lodging, and that provided a source of revenue for village residents, who ran boardinghouses or hotels for the bathhouse guests. The Terry Hotel, DeMar Cottage, Todd Boarding House and rooms in the homes of R.B. Merrill, C.E. Tuttle, Minnie Wood, Celey Kingsley, Algy Kingsley, Jennie Morley and Laura Blanchard offered lodging options. The Davis Restaurant was a popular dining spot for these guests. Overall, the economic impact on Andover Village was estimated at $200,000 annually in 1923.

The Lost Princess

Anderson's bathhouse was a prophecy of Andover's future in water and tourism. His brochure proclaimed that "you should spend your vacation at these beneficial baths" and that the area offered "good hotels, boarding houses and cottages; fine water; beautiful parks and shade trees; good railroad accommodations."

Ten years after his death, Anderson's words proved prophetic with construction of the Pymatuning Dam and resulting reservoir. It would offer tourists the amenities of fine water, parks, shade trees, cottages and something the bathhouse could not provide—fishing and boating.

This lake, which straddles the border between Ohio and Pennsylvania, hides history rather well. Few people are still alive who recall the farms that slipped beneath the rising waters when the dam gates were closed, but the old maps testify to the many property owners who had to be bought out in order to create the flood-control project. Indeed, a portion of an entire

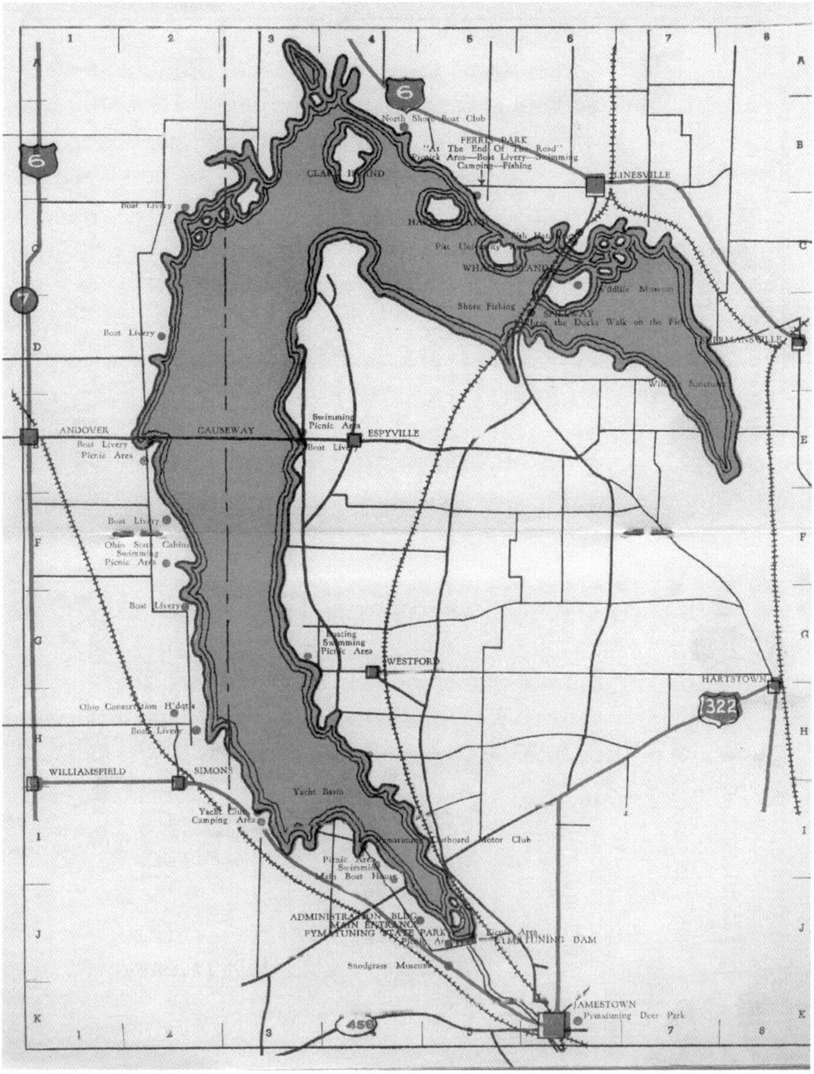

A map of the Pymatuning Reservoir published in the 1950s shows the odd shape of the lake that formed after the dam gates were closed. The lake straddles Ohio and Pennsylvania. *Ashtabula County Historical Society collection.*

town, Simon, was sacrificed in order to save the residents and businesses of the Shenango and Beaver Valleys the heartache and misery of periodic flooding and drought.

It took more than two decades for Pennsylvania and Ohio to get everything in order. The lake would cover 16,720 acres. Much of this was swamp and thick forest to begin with, but it was not unproductive.[30] The muck was incredibly rich and well suited for root crops. Some farmers grew celery bunches and cauliflower weighing fifteen pounds each. But the soil's best crop was onions, which were mildly flavored and huge—up to eighteen inches across. Yields were four to eight hundred bushels per acre, and a bushel brought $3.50. By 1917, the fields around this swamp were producing one-third of the onions in the United States. Linesville, Pennsylvania, was the nation's onion capital.

The Pymatuning Land Company was formed to acquire the Ohio land that would be covered by the lake. Eventually, eight thousand acres in Ohio would be cleared. The work got under way in 1932 and employed around seven thousand men who slept and ate in tents until the work was done.

The workers were organized into crews, each one assigned a five-hundred-foot-wide strip to the high-water line on either side. Some strips were as long as two miles, and up to eight crews would work alongside one another at one time.

They worked throughout the summer and winter, harvesting and removing whatever valuable timber could be salvaged. Everything else was burned. Barns, granaries, coops, sheds and homesteads also had to be cleared. The mantra was "Pick up and burn everything that might float later on." According to the *History of Pymatuning Reservoir, 1909–1934*,

> *The common practice in clearing was to place logs in a pile, like matches in a box. A fire was started with brush in the center of the pile. It was a common sight to see wet logs burning in the middle while water would be squirting from either end. Many looked upon the burning as an economic loss to lumber, but it was practically impossible to get the logs from the swamp.*

Follow-up crews confirmed the quality of the work done by the initial crews and removed any troublesome stumps and unburned logs. Traces of history emerged as the underbrush was cleared. There were places where the soil had burned to a depth of several feet, and at one point, an old log road was discovered under the muck. These roads, much like the corduroy road of Blodgett's Turnpike, were the only way of traversing the swamp. Even then, travelers had to be alert to sections being washed out by a heavy rain or simply disappearing in the muck. The road discovered by the workers had logs about two inches in diameter, about one-fourth of their original diameter.

Amazingly, this sweep of the swamp did not recover what many consider to be Pymatuning's greatest mystery: a wooden ship that became bogged down in the swamp and was left to decay.

The story of this phenomenon occurs in historical writings from both sides of the lake. Eyewitnesses described it as a big boat, sixty to one hundred feet long and twelve feet wide, and its location as about two miles southeast of the Linesville spillway.

According to the Linesville, Pennsylvania Historical Society, the most common explanation for the boat is that it was one of a fleet of four commissioned to bring Spanish princess Sanzavora from New Orleans to Canada, where she was to marry a French prince. According to legend, a marriage had been arranged to bind the royal houses of Bourbon and Castile. The responsibility of the journey fell on the princess, who was expected to travel from New Orleans to the prince of France in the Quebec country. Why they attempted this trip through a barely explored country in the late seventeenth century is beyond comprehension. But without that scenario, we have no story, and without the story, there can be no boat.

The princess was aboard the largest of the four boats, which were laden with a dowry of gold and jewels worth 100,000 doubloons. Also on board

Hidden under the Pymatuning Reservoir are the remains of an old boat or two, possibly of Spanish origin, if one believes the legend of Princess Sanzavora. *Author's collection.*

was a cache of muskets and soldiers to guard the treasure. The ships left New Orleans and traveled up the Mississippi River. As the vessels passed French forts, the princess was honored as the "Bride of France." At the area that would become the Ohio River town of Marietta, she received her last recognition from white men.

Native Americans reported seeing the boats heading up the Beaver River at its confluence with the Ohio. Nothing was seen or heard from the princess and her entourage after that. The assumption is that they made it as far as the Pymatuning swamp, got stuck in the notorious quicksand and were swallowed, except for the one boat.

Given the status of parties involved, and the size of the dowry, there ought to be a historical record of such a failed journey. However, a researcher at the Historic New Orleans Collection could not find a scrap of documentation among either historical or folklore resources. And "Princess Sanzavora" is one of the few phrases that can be Googled and not generate one match.

Nevertheless, there are nineteenth-century eyewitnesses who claimed to have seen the vessel in their explorations of the swamp. An M.P. Sargent gave this description in 1891:

> *In 1850 John Hadlock, now of Ashtabula, Ohio, in company with John McMurty of Harmonsburg, Pa., visited the Pymatuning Swamp, situated in Crawford County, Pa. At a point where the Pymatuning Creek and another stream come together, they boarded an old vessel (which had been known to exist there) for the purpose of obtaining some of its timber as a relic.*
>
> *They succeeded in getting a piece of plank from the deck of the vessel near the bow, from which McMurty made two canes, which are now in the possession of his family. Mr. McMurty died in 1885 at the age of 102 years.*
>
> *The vessel lies about twenty feet from the channel of the Pymatuning Creek, overgrown with moss, birch and tamarack trees from four to 18 inches in diameter. The bow stern stuck up about two feet from the mucky earth. On the opposite side of the creek from where this vessel lay, is an old fort, embankments thrown up in a semi-circle form, like breastworks. And within this semi-circle, Spanish coins have been found, and trees were standing, some of which were two feet in diameter.*

The late Catherine Ellsworth, in her *Historical Sketches of Ashtabula County*, had another take on the story that had been related to her by an unnamed Conneaut man. He claimed the boat was built by Pittsburgh traders who sailed it up the Beaver and Shenango Rivers during a time of high water. The boat was dated to the Revolutionary War.

Could this tale be connected to the skeletons found, faces down, their finger bones still wrapped about the rusty musket barrels, near the Ashtabula River? Or were the occupants of these boats able to make it as far as the bluff at Ashtabula Township, where they succumbed to illness or harsh weather and were buried overlooking the river?

The last documented report of the boat came from the early 1930s, when Jamestown, Pennsylvania residents Abe Palmanteer, John Blair and Lee Mason reported seeing the vessel, whose wood was foreign to the region. Additionally, it was held together with copper rivets.

And then the dam gates were closed, and the impounded waters spread across the swamp and lay to rest its legends.

Notes

The Road to History

1. The exact route of the Old Girdled Road has been a topic of study and dispute among regional historians for years. As to its course in Kelloggsville, it is believed that Church Street was built on the road.
2. Most sources, including Blodgett's grave marker, spell his name with two *t*'s; however, in the Ashtabula County census records, only one was used.
3. Few roads in Ashtabula County have had as many names as this one. Originally a Native American path, this road passed through West Williamsfield, West Andover, Leon and on to Kelloggsville, according to historian Walter Jack. It became known as State Road prior to Blodgett's venture. Jack states that Blodgett built the turnpike in 1807, but that is inconsistent with other accounts of his arrival in the township. It is likely that Blodgett's role was that of improver of the existing path. However, his improvements did not include a bridge; stagecoaches still had to ford the west branch of the Ashtabula River before entering Ferguson's Settlement. In 1816, a road was authorized from "Pierpont to Ferguson's Bridge in Monroe," suggesting both the existence of a bridge and the overall improvement of this section of the road. Stanhope-Kelloggsville also has been referred to as the "Old Salt Road," although this designation does not align the road with the "Old Salt Road" as it exists in Williamsfield Township.
4. This tavern was built for Harvey Sperry on the west side of the turnpike and had twenty-two rooms. A frame structure, it was reduced in size when

the stagecoach industry fizzled and renamed the "Smith Mansion." The old tavern, in the twentieth century, was used as a grocery and home; today, it is a private residence, a testimony to Blodgett's construction skills.

5. In 1820, the population of Cleveland was 606, and the population of Ashtabula County was 7,369. Thirty years later, Cuyahoga County had 47,740 persons, but Ashtabula County had only 28,724. The coming of the railroads two years later would greatly contribute to the widening gap.
6. Sarepta Marie Blodgett married Joseph Leland Haywood of Massachusetts. The Haywoods departed for Salt Lake City, Utah, with the Willard Richards Company, on July 3, 1848, and arrived on October 10, 1848. Sarepta Marie died in Salt Lake City on December 4, 1881.
7. After the loss of his distillery, Caleb Blodgett headed west to government land south of Chicago. At Meacham's Grove, Blodgett started all over with a log cabin and, with the help of his sons, broke a large number of acres for crops. The natural resources of timber, prairie and water power revived Blodgett. Although a squatter, Blodgett pursued improvements as if he had clear title to the land east of the Rock River. He soon had a relatively luxurious house and mill to cut the lumber for the homes that he was certain would follow in this "Eden." Blodgett had acquired a claim from an old Canadian, Thiebault, who granted "three looks" in every direction from Blodgett's cabin. The New England Emigrating Company soon purchased one-third of the claim Blodgett had thus acquired. The settlement filled rapidly and became known as Beloit, Wisconsin, where Caleb Blodgett is buried and duly honored as its founder. His tavern in Kelloggsville no longer physically bears his name; the plaque that once declared "Blodgett's Tavern" disappeared long ago. However, there is a "Caleb Avenue" in Kelloggsville, and old-timers still refer to this portion of Stanhope-Kelloggsville as the "Turnpike." In another generation, that story will be forgotten, hidden under the macadam like the rotting wood fibers of the corduroy road itself.
8. Some sources spell the surname "Meade." Walter Jack gives his first name as "Darius," but the census records confirm the presence of "Abel Mead," the name also used by Paul Hakala in his account of Steamburg.
9. While Mead's plan sounds far-fetched, it was just one of several attempts to link Lake Erie to the Ohio River via either existing waterways or through a canal. And it was not just hucksters like Mead who had these plans. The Jones and McLaughin Steel Company purchased a large tract of land on Wheeler Creek in Geneva Township (today the west side of the state park) because a lake-to-river canal was envisioned. Wheeler's flow is about as heavy as that of the west branch. Surveys, by well-credentialed firms and dreamers, were made of the Ashtabula and other Ashtabula County waterways in hopes of finding that route to the Ohio River and

Pittsburgh. During the 1960s, the proposal was heavily debated. But common sense prevailed, and the boondoggle was never built. Had it been, the county would have even more history hidden under water.

10. J.E. Baker was a son of George and Hannah Baker. George Baker came to the United States in 1851 and worked as a tailor in Painesville. John E. learned the cigar-making trade as a young man and pursued that for twenty years prior to moving to Andover, where he operated his store for more than forty-five years. He served as the township clerk and the clerk to the school district for thirty-five years.

11. This lane was once the Stanhope-Kelloggsville Road, which was moved to the east a few hundred yards after the railroad came through. The relocation prevented two railroad crossings and, thus, made travel safer and more expedient, especially given the number of trains in those days and the fact that the train stopped at Stanhope, which would have blocked the highway.

12. Great effort was put forth by the county's agricultural community to produce desirable butter. With crude methods and no refrigeration, the settlers' early efforts were referred to as tasteless "Ohio grease."

FAITH

13. Austinburg was settled just two years prior with the arrival of Judge Eliphalet Austin and seven others. During their first summer in the new settlement, the three families of this little colony gathered every Sabbath to worship. Lacking a religious leader, a sermon was read. It is said that Badger preached the first sermon ever delivered in the county or Reserve in August 1800 at Austinburg.

14. A Pentecostal Holiness congregation emerged from a series of tent meetings held in Ashtabula in 1928. Appalachian Pentecostals wanted local autonomy, something the denomination did not offer. Also, the church used piano and organ, but the Appalachians were more accustomed to guitars in their worship services. There also was a Finnish charismatic church where speaking in tongues was practiced.

UNDERGROUND RAILROAD

15. There is debate about who built this house. The documentation provided for the National Register of Historic Places attributes it to John Henderson, a tailor, who lived in the house with his wife, three children and an apprentice. Perhaps the myriad spools are a nod to his line of work.

16. Giddings was sent back to his district, the Sixteenth, when the House voted 125 to 69 on March 22, 1842, to censure its peer for violating the gag rule, which prevented the representatives from acknowledging antislavery petitions/resolutions while in session. Giddings broke the rule by introducing a series of resolutions that defended a slave rebellion aboard a ship sailing between Virginia and the Bahamas. After the vote was taken, Giddings resigned in protest. But voters held a special election and returned their abolitionist congressman to his post, where he remained until 1859.
17. Whether or not Giddings was aware of Brown's plan to capture the federal arsenal at Harpers Ferry, Virginia, is unclear. When Giddings testified before the Senate committee that investigated John Brown's raid, he admitted to the appointment with Brown in his office and that he had arranged for Brown to speak at the Congregational church in Jefferson. Giddings told the committee that a collection of more than $10 and less than $20 was raised at that event. While Giddings probably did not have any connection to the raid, some Southerners saw him as a great threat, and a Richmond, Virginia newspaper promised to pay $10,000 to whoever could deliver Giddings to that city alive; $5,000 was offered for his dead body. Such was the intense hatred of this man who refused to compromise on the slavery issue.
18. M.W. Beede was one of the county's most adventurous and energetic men of the nineteenth century. He was born on August 28, 1839, in New Hampshire and left home at the age of ten to come to the Western Reserve. A Black String, he served in Company D, Nineteenth Ohio Infantry, upon Lincoln's call for troops in 1861 and fought at Rich Mountain in Virginia. A disability kept him from reenlisting, but he assisted the war effort by manufacturing boat oars for use by the military. In his retirement years, he traveled extensively and, in July 1915, became the first white man to climb Mount Massive, Colorado's highest mountain.
19. The loss of the pistol is collaborated by a story that appeared in the *Shepherdstown (Virginia) Register* on October 22, 1859. It related how Cook and Stephens visited the residence of Colonel Lewis Washington more than a fortnight prior to the insurrection and learned of both the pistol and a sword in Washington's possession. The men returned during the raid, captured Washington and demanded the pistol and sword, the latter carried by John Brown Sr. during the time he was surrounded in the engine house. The sword was recovered after the engine house was stormed; the pistol, however, was still missing as of the time the story was published.
20. Barclay's brother, Edwin, also present at the raid, was executed the same day as John Brown and two others, Shields Green and John A. Copeland. Barclay joined the Union army and was killed in the Platte Bridge Railroad Tragedy. The bushwhacker attack killed between seventeen and twenty

and injured one hundred. Confederate partisans sabotaged a wooden trestle over the Platte River, and on September 3, 1861, the locomotive, freight cars, baggage and mail cars and two passenger cars with men, women and children aboard fell into the shallow river.

Mounds, Graveyards and Reverend Spalding

21. As of January 2015, the location of *Le Griffon*, the sailing ship that Sieur de La Salle launched to find the Northwest Passage to the Orient, was supposedly in Lake Michigan, but its discoverers were not disclosing its location to the media.
22. As intriguing as these stories of giants are to residents of the Western Reserve, these relics have been found elsewhere in North America. *The Ancient Giants Who Ruled America* by Richard J. Dewhurst pulls together numerous accounts of these giants garnered from newspapers and local histories. Ashtabula County's giants are part of this collection, and the reader who is interested in the theories and conspiracies surrounding this subject would be well served and entertained by this and other books devoted exclusively to the subject.
23. Often spelled "Spaulding" in older literature.
24. Henry Lake, Solomon Spalding's business partner, stated, according to Henry Howe's *History of Ohio*, that Ridgon was

> *a very eccentric character, with an unbalanced mind, and somewhat of a monomaniac upon the subject of the Bible...He became very intimate with Mr. Lambdin, was often in the printing office, where all the manuscripts which were candidates for publication, were on the shelves. For three years he deemed it* [h]*is duty to abandon all other employment, even preaching, that he might devote his whole time to the study of the Bible...*
>
> *This man, looking over manuscripts, fell upon Mr. Spalding's, which* [he] *read and re-read with the greatest interest. It was peculiarly adapted to his half-crazed state of mind. He became so much absorbed in the work that he copied it, as he himself frequently stated.*

Disguises

25. It was discovered a year later that Elizabeth had not been sworn in, and she and Clara were officially sworn into service by the provost marshal on October 10, 1864. Her service to the Union ended shortly thereafter.

TINKER HOLLOW

26. Ohio had seventy-two iron furnaces in 1840. They produced 35,236 tons of cast iron that year but required 104,312 tons of charcoal in the process. An acre of virgin forest yielded about 40.0 cords of wood, and 5.84 cords were required for 1 ton of iron. Much of the virgin forests in the Western Reserve were felled for building plank and corduroy roads and making charcoal, not for houses, barns, schools and churches.
27. At that time, bolts and nuts were produced as matched items; standardization did not exist among the manufacturers.
28. The last reference to a Tinker mowing machine being seen in public was at the 1896 centennial parade for Conneaut.
29. Tinker was not the only Ashtabula County manufacturer with a secret recipe for metal. In North Kingsville, during the early part of the twentieth century, the Palmer Company allegedly had a secret formula for the metal it used in the spigots manufactured by the firm. The formula was inscribed on a board in the bedroom of a house that the Palmer family owned and rented. The house was razed and the formula lost when the last man to work at the factory died.

UNMARKED GRAVES

30. The story is told of an Annette Smith Clark who wandered into these woods with a two-year-old child and got lost. She ended up climbing a tree to escape a panther and spent two harrowing nights in the tree, child in arms, while the panther paced below. She and the child were rescued by two men who were piloting a raft on the Shenango River.

Bibliography

Abbott, John Stevens Cabot. *The History of the State of Ohio: From Discover of the Great Valley to the Present Time*. Detroit: Northwestern Publishing Company, 1875.

Allison, Grace C. "The Western Reserve's Civil War Spy." *Western Reserve Magazine*, November–December 1981.

Ashtabula County Genealogical Society. *Ashtabula County History, Then and Now: A History of the People of the County by the People of the County*. Dallas, TX: Taylor Publishing Co., 1985.

Ashtabula Star Beacon. "Ashtabula's Mushroom King." August 26, 2012.

———. "Gould." January 2, 1971.

———. "A History: The Port of Ashtabula." December 17, 1961.

———. "A Lady Spy." March 7, 1997.

———. "Left Handed Monkey Wrench…" June 18, 1947

———. "Legendary Iron: Tinker Secret … Never Revealed." February 17, 1998.

———. "Legend of the Metal Grave Markers." February 18, 1998.

———. "Legends of Tinker Hollow." February 16, 1998.

———. "Legends of Tinker's Hollow." October 30, 2011.

———. "Of Spools and Slaves." April 9, 2001.

———. "Steamburg Was 'Center' of Lumber Industry." July 1, 1976.

———. "3 Masted Ships on Creek at Steamburg." October 25, 1965.

———. "(Tinker Items) Acquired by Historical Society." October 14, 1971

Ashtabula Weekly Telegraph. "Accident at Tinker Hollow!" August 27, 1870

Badger, Joseph. "Ohio History Central." http://www.ohiohistorycentral.org/w/Badger,_Joseph.

Bogue, ed. "A Station on the Underground Railroad." *Ashtabula County Historical Society Quarterly Bulletin*, December 15, 1964, 1–3.

Brown, John, Jr. "John Brown Jr. to John Brown." Letter. Kansas Historical Society. http://www.kansasmemory.org/item/4731/text.

Cheney, Frank J. *A Life of Unity, and Other Stories*. Toledo, OH: Blade Printing & Paper Co., 1901.

The Church of Jesus Christ of Latter-Day Saints. "Willard Richards Company." http://history.lds.org/overlandtravels/companyPioneers?lang=eng&companyId=2.

Cincinnati Daily Gazette. "Death of a Singular Character." June 23, 1871.

"The City of Cleveland." *Harper's New Monthly Magazine* (March 1886).

(Cleveland) Leader and Herald. "Spalding." March 9, 1886.

Cleveland Plain Dealer. "Like Mushrooms? Ohio Grows World's Choicest." November 17, 1937.

Cleveland Plain Dealer Magazine. "Man-Made Lake Is Ohio's New Playground." October 13, 1935.

Cleveland Plain Dealer Pictorial Magazine. "Old Manuscript by Conneaut Pastor…Now Rests Behind Locked Doors in Oberlin College Library." March 5, 1960.

Colling, May, comp. *Early Harbor History and Bridge Street*. Geneva, OH: Ashtabula County Genealogical Society, 2014.

Concise Dictionary of Christianity in America. Downers Grove, IL: Intervarsity Press, 1995.

DeRogatis, Amy. *Moral Geography: Maps, Missionaries and the American Frontier*. New York: Columbia University Press, 2003.

Dewhurst, Richard J. *The Ancient Giants Who Ruled America*. Rochester, VT: Bear and Company, 2014.

Elkhart Weekly Review. "The Funny Man at Conneaut." July 13, 1871.

Ellsworth, Catherine Trapp. *Ellsworth's Historical Sketches of Ashtabula County, Ohio*. N.p.: self-published, 1988. Available at Platt R. Spencer Memorial Archives & Special Collections, Geneva, Ohio.

(Erie, PA) Sunday Times. "Underground Railroad." June 12, 1949.

Fairburn, Noreen Sippola, ed. *My Father Spoke Finglish at Work*. Kent, OH: Kent State University Press, 2007.

Feather, Carl E. *Mountain People in a Flat Land*. Athens: Ohio University Press, 1997.

Fuller, Robert. *Underground to Freedom*. Jefferson, OH: Gazette Printing, 1977.

A History of the Pymatuning Reservoir, 1909–1934. Available at the Ashtabula County Historical Society Walter Jack Research Library, Geneva-on-the-Lake, Ohio.

Howe, Eber, D. *Moronism Unvailed.* Painesville, OH: Telegraph Press, 1834.

Howe, Henry. *Historical Collections of Ohio in Two Volumes.* Cincinnati, OH: C.J. Krehbiel & Co., 1902.

Hubbard House Underground Railroad Museum. "The Hubbard Family." http://www.hubbardhouseugrrmuseum.org/about-us.

Jack, Walter. "History of Ashtabula County." Undated manuscript available at the Ashtabula County Historical Society Walter Jack Memorial Research Library, Geneva-on-the-Lake, Ohio.

Jefferson Gazette. "The Changing Scene: Hot Springs Bath House." January 2, 1962.

———. "Dr. Anderson Tells of Practice." December 1, 1923.

———. "M.W. Beede Tells of the Lenox Black Strings." March 19, 1914.

———. "Walter Jack Describes Origin of the Names of Ashtabula County Townships." February 20, 1953.

———. "West Andover Woolen Mill." March 11, 1992.

———. "When Iron Was Made at Conneaut." February 2, 1924.

———. "Writes Story of Tinkers' Hollow." July 19, 1927.

Jones, Loyal. *The Roots of Appalachian Christianity.* Lexington: University Press of Kentucky, 2001.

Jones, Robert Leslie. *History of Agriculture in Ohio to 1880.* Kent, OH: Kent State University Press, 1983.

Kelloggsville Bicentennial Committee. *Kelloggsville: 1799–1999.* Self-published. Available in the resource room of the Jefferson Historical Society, Jefferson, Ohio.

Lake, D.J. *Atlas of Ashtabula County.* Philadephia: Titus, Simmons & Titus, 1874.

Lampson, Chet. *John Brown and Ashtabula County: An Ohio Story.* Jefferson, OH: Jefferson Gazette, 1955.

Land, Mary. "John Brown's Ohio Environment." *Ohio Archaeological and Historical Quarterly* 57. http://publications.ohiohistory.org.

Large, Moina W. *History of Ashtabula County, Ohio, in Two Volumes.* Vol. 1. Topeka, KS: Historical Publishing Co., 1924.

Leonard, George, E., ed. *Historical Papers Concerning the Ashtabula Baptist Association 1817–1907.* 1907. Available at the Ashtabula County Historical Society, Geneva-on-the-Lake, Ohio.

Lupold, Harry F., and Gladys Haddad, eds. *Ohio's Western Reserve: A Regional Reader.* Kent, OH: Kent State University Press, 1988.

"Manuscript of Solomon Spalding and the Book of Mormon." *National Magazine: A Monthly Journal of American History* 4 (May 1886–October 1886).

Matthews, Alfred. *Ohio and Her Western Reserve*. New York: D. Appleton & Co., 1902.

McCrory. "East Side Home Built in Early 1800s by Eccentric." *Conneaut News Herald*. Undated clip, collection of Judy Pallutch, Ashtabula, Ohio.

Milwaukee Journal. "Lincoln Letter, Always Carried by Woman Spy, Comes to Light." June 24, 1960.

Neal A. Maxwell Institute for Religious Scholarship. "The Historical Case Against Sidney Rigdon's Authorship of the Book of Mormon." http://publications.maxwellinstitute.byu.edu/fullscreen/?pub=1462&index=8.

New York Times. "The Harper's Ferry Affair." March 29, 1860.

———. "The Late Capt. John R. Stanhope." January 28, 1873.

Ohio Civil War Central. "Burrows' Battery of Ohio Volunteer Artillery." http://www.ohiocivilwarcentral.com/entry.php?rec=726.

Patterson, Helen. "A Short History of the Clyde Iron Furnace." *Ashtabula County Historical Society Quarterly Bulletin*, December 15, 1965, 1–7.

Reminisces of the Cleveland Light Artillery. Cleveland, OH: Cleveland Printing Co., 1906. Available at the Ashtabula County Historical Society Walter Jack Research Library, Geneva-on-the-Lake, Ohio.

Robbins, D.P. *The City of Ashtabula*. N.p., 1893. Available at the Ashtabula County Historical Society, Geneva-on-the-Lake, Ohio.

Rotundo, Barbara. "White Bronze Memorials Recall a Forgotten Era." *MB News*, January 1998.

Shawnee Dispatch. "1862 Raid Gave Woman a Passion for the Union" October 19, 2005.

Shepherdstown Register. "Slave Insurrection at Harpers Ferry." October 22, 1859. http://www.wvculture.org/history/jbexhibit/shepherdstownregraid.html.

"Slevey K. Blodgett." *Portrait & Biographical Record Winnebago & Boone Cos*. Chicago: Biographical Pub. Co., 1882.

"Spalding Manuscript." Oberlin College Archives. http://www.oberlin.edu/archive/holdings/finding/RG30/SG28/history.html.

Spalding, Solomon. *The Manuscript Found*. Reprint from original. Salt Lake, UT: Deseret News Company, 1886.

Spellman, Marlin J. *History of Andover and Andover Township, Ashtabula County, Ohio*. N.p.: self-published, 1976. Available at Andover Public Library, Andover, Ohio.

———. *A History of Leon, Richmond Township*. N.p.: self-published, May 1976. Available at Ashtabula County Historical Society collection, Geneva-on-the-Lake, Ohio.

Spencer, Platt R. *Record of the Historical and Philosophical Society of Ashtabula County, Ohio*. Available at Ashtabula County Historical Society collection, Geneva-on-the-Lake, Ohio.

Stewart, John Struthers. *History of Northeastern Ohio*. Indianapolis: Historical Publishing Co., 1935.

Sullivan, Ken, ed. *The West Virginia Encyclopedia*. Charleston: West Virginia Humanities Council, 2006.

Terhune, Albert Payson. *A Book of Famous Dogs*. New York: Sun Dial Press, Inc., 1939.

Tinker, A.W. Letter to Walter Jack. August 13, 1955. Available at Platt R. Spencer Memorial Archives & Special Collections, Geneva, Ohio.

Town of Floyd History. "Historical Society." http://town.floyd.ny.us/content/history.

Uncle Dale's Readings. "Misc. Ohio Newspapers 1910–1999 Archives." http://www.sidneyrigdon.com/dbroadhu/oh/miscoh07.htm.

U.S. House of Representatives. "Historical Highlights: The House Censured…Joshua R. Giddings of Ohio." http://history.house.gov/HistoricalHighlight/Detail/36674.

VanCourt, Jim. Interview by the author.

Weekly Telegraph Newspapers. *History of Ashtabula Township by Reverend John Hall*. 1870. Reprint, Jefferson, OH: Ashtabula County Historical Society, compilation 2001.

Western Historical Company. *The History of Rock County, Wisconsin: Its Early Settlement, Growth, Development, Resources, Etc*. Chicago: Western Historical Company, 1879.

Wikipedia. "Ashery." http://en.wikipedia.org/wiki/Ashery.

———. "Bog Iron." http://en.wikipedia.org/wiki/Bog_iron.

———. "Col. Stephen Moulton (Soldier)." http://en.wikipedia.org/wiki/Stephen_Moulton_(soldier).

———. "Spalding-Ridgon Theory of Book of Mormon Authorship." http://en.wikipedia.org/wiki/Spalding%E2%80%93Rigdon_theory_of_Book_of_Mormon_authorship.

Williamsfield Memories. N.p.: self-published. Available at the resource room of the Jefferson Historical Society, Jefferson, Ohio.

Williams, William W. *History of Ashtabula County*. Philadelphia: Williams Brothers, 1878.

About the Author

Carl E. Feather is a writer, photographer and videographer with roots in Appalachia and a home in Ohio's Western Reserve. A lodging tax administrator for the Ashtabula County Board of Commissioners, Carl is involved in the development of new tourism attractions. This is his fourth book and second with The History Press.